SPECTER

SPECTER

RANDY & BRIAN DELANEY

Published by Spines
ISBN 979-8-89383-488-8

CONTENTS

FOREWORD

WHY ARE THEY CHEERING THIS MAN?

There have long been stories of men throughout history who operated from the shadows, seemingly beyond the reach of law. Men who could be described as part angel and part demon; their loyalties clearly to their family, their friends, their country and to the oppressed. Men like Wes Lindsell who strikes from the shadows in defense of the common man.

During a brilliant career in the United States' Army's Special Forces Group as a crack team member of the Criminal Investigation Division (CID), there was nobody in the military beyond Wes' authority. When he finally retires into anonymity, it's not for very long. Circumstances in the crumbling fabric of modern-day America's legal system lure him back into action to pursue justice on the civilian front and root out core corruption from the street punk level to the highest law offices and to the liberal court justices.

His pursuits take him across the Ohio Valley, to the coal mining area of Kentucky, the hardened streets of Southside Chicago, and to the detritus of inner-city Detroit, before finally focusing on the volatile southwest border and a confrontation with the cartels. But, as Wes soon learns, when a woman becomes involved, that path of righteousness can become very murky.

"Written laws are like spider's webs; they will catch, it is true, the weak and the poor, but would be torn in pieces by the rich and the powerful."

- Anacharsis, sixth century Scythian prince.

CHAPTER 1

MIDDLETON, OHIO

WES LINDSELL WAS STILL BRISTLING with anger as he eased his classic burgundy 1966 Pontiac GTO into his driveway after an evening out with his pals at their favorite sports pub. The night was still young and it had been good fun watching their beloved Cleveland Browns take down their nemesis, the Baltimore Ravens, that Sunday afternoon to earn a spot in the NFL playoffs. It was only after the game, when the conversation ranged to topics other than football, that Wes was reminded of the story about a father who, after murdering his two year old son in a drunken rage several months ago, would be released from prison to join his wife and remaining kids for Christmas. This tragedy had occurred two months prior and Wes had been moved enough to do some preliminary scouting at the time and now that the criminal's release was imminent he was ready to set the wheels in motion.

Wes was a product of his small, upper middle eastern town upbringing which still held on to morality, ethical behavior and a good sense of community as guiding principles in life. His father had been a good man, a hard working welder by trade who had earned enough to meet the simple family needs. Mom could have stepped right out of an "Ozzie & Harriet" episode. A dedicated housewife, she even worked a few hours every week at the local five and dime so that Wes and his younger sister Dana could experience luxuries like going to the state fair every year, enjoy an amusement park, or make a trip to an all-you-can-eat buffet on their birthdays. The rules of the household were both strict and fair back then. You lived by them, you pitched in your fair share, and you didn't question authority figures. Not your parents, not your teachers, not the local police, and certainly not Father Kerin at the local Catholic school. And if you missed his mass on Sunday then you had better be prepared to spend the day at home. Dad's thinking was that If you didn't feel well enough for church on Sunday morning then you didn't feel well enough to do anything else that day either. Sister Teresa at the school had actually said one day in Sunday School that it was written that way in the bible somewhere, but Wes never really believed her at the time.

That was the black and white world that Wes grew up in, so every time he heard a story about senseless killings, especially of innocent babes, pedophilia, and beatings of those who could not defend themselves, he became incensed. When he had first learned that a prominent liberal court justice and a shady district attorney were constructing a deal to allow a worthless animal like this murdering father to walk free, well it made him nauseous. Every day stories such as these reflected the continued collapse of the America he grew up in. The details were often buried somewhere deep in section B of the local paper, almost as an afterthought. Where was the public outrage? When had it become acceptable to just grow immune to these atrocities and simply turn the page to the sports section with faint regard for the victim or condemn the complicit justice system?

As Wes steered his GTO to a gentle stop in his driveway, he stepped out and admired his retirement present to himself with great satisfaction. His anger abated as he ran his hand along the multi-colored trim of his 38' MountainAir Luxury RV Coach. He was nearly his usual calm self again as he turned his thoughts towards his next step in life. His long career with the U.S. Army CID Agency (Criminal Investigation Division) had been successful and after 36 years he was enjoying the first few weeks of retirement and the freedoms that it offered. He had saved and invested wisely, lived well within his means, and his only slight misstep was a nasty divorce a number of years back in which he blamed himself to a large degree. He was completely immersed in his investigation work back then. The missus eventually found a man who took the time to pay her the attention she required.

Much of the American way of life had changed during Wes' adult years, and not much of it for the better. Gangs, guns, drugs, political greed and violence dominated his world for too long. His distaste for all the crime and cruelty grew with each passing year and now as he stood in his driveway eyeing his prize RV, a smile slowly spread across his face. He had been planning his escape for some time and with his retirement at hand he was ready to set that plan in motion. The RV had been loaded up with 150 gallons of diesel earlier that morning and tomorrow would be the first day of his new life. A life which would become dramatically changed.

CHAPTER 2

THE OHIO RIVER VALLEY

EARLY THE NEXT morning Wes blinked himself awake and stared at the familiar surroundings of his room for what would be the last time in a long while. He slipped on his Minnesota Vikings sweatshirt and faded denim jeans, made his first cup of coffee for the day, and sat on his front steps to enjoy it. It was not yet 6:30 a.m. and the city was blessed by a crisp breeze in these late days of fall. He occasionally cast his eyes to the sky and watched the strands of gold and red paint the horizon as the sun began its ascent. He finished his coffee, buttoned down the house and was on his way within the hour.

The Ohio River Valley is a fertile basin of more than 200,000 square miles which stretch across 6 states. It was formed by the confluence of the Allegheny & Monongahela Rivers and more than 25 million people live along the Ohio River Basin. Autumn blesses this magnificent landscape with a rich carpet of crimsons, yellows, golds and chestnut tones. The hills were green and rolling and It was this remarkable vista that greeted Wes on Monday morning as he drove south along Interstate 71, crossing the great state of Ohio and soon over the

Ohio River as he entered Kentucky. He lowered his driver's side window and breathed deeply, taking in the crisp fall air and the taste of the rich outdoors. He preferred the fresh air, hot or not, as it helped focus his mind on his mission. He was indeed a new man today with a new found freedom.

Wes Lindsell was exactly six feet one and one half inches tall in his stockinged feet. He knew this because his former employer, the United States Army, was very precise at measuring its personnel. He was 212 pounds which, on the Army's height-to-weight-to-age scale was considered ideal. If there was an ounce of fat on the man it would take a micro-scope to find it. His muscles were long and ropy and even now in his 50s he remained toned. This was not by happenstance, but rather by a discipline that he never surrendered. He ate sensibly without being prudish about it and he exercised daily, continuing to push himself even as the years advanced and the muscles protested a little more. Wes had joined the Army for adventure as a young man and had signed on for Jump School in Fort Benning, GA where he earned his silver parachute wings. His drive throughout basic training, advanced infantry training, and later jump school did not go unnoticed. He was invited to try out for Special Forces Training School and successfully earned his Green Beret a year later. He had that right mix of brain and brawn that the Army loved, and his commanding officers were all pushing him towards West Point. However Wes didn't much like desks and preferred to be out in the field with the grunts doing the dirty work. "I like where I am and I like the way I got here" Wes often answered when asked why he didn't chase after Captain's bars or even General's stars. After a couple of years of leading new recruits in PT (personal training) and rifle marksmanship, Wes recognized that a peace time Army could be pretty dull for a grunt soldier when there was no battlefield. He filed for the Army's Central Investigative

Division (CID) and became a special agent, spending the remainder of his distinguished career investigating homicides and high profile crimes by military personnel, even when those crossed over into the civilian side.

Judge Brammar was a former civil rights lawyer whose radical views were embraced by the left. He represented the new breed of reformers who campaigned on reducing mass incarceration and the elimination of bail. These types tend to prefer such alternative punishments as treatment programs, reduced prosecution of low level crimes, counseling and substance abuse programs. Brammar had quickly become one of the prominent figures in this movement on a national scale along with Philadelphia District Attorney Larry Krasner, Illinois State Attorney Kim Foxx and San Francisco District Attorney Chesa Boudin who learned about prison as a child visiting his parents, Weather Underground radicals Kathy Boudin and David Gilbert in prison. It was Brammar who paved the way for son-slayer Steve Kadell to enjoy a reduced sentence and return home to his family for the holidays. The Judge wasn't hearing any cases this week so Wes knew where to find him. He was, if nothing else, a creature of habit and when the Judge wasn't adjudicating he was likely at his country club working on his respectable golf game. He had been playing with the same foursome for more than a decade and it was his routine to have lunch in the Men's Grill, bolstered by a Tanqueray Martini up, dirty, and then make his way to the club's driving range where he methodically hit an entire stack of balls before his round. He was a competitive sort and took great precision with his golf practice, starting with the short irons and progressing to the driver before teeing it up with his buddies.

Wes had the judge's routine committed to memory. He had scouted out the country club earlier with the same precision that he investigated his CID cases. He parked his RV on the periphery of the expansive club parking lot so as not to draw undue attention. He was dressed casually as were most golfers; collared polo shirt, garish slacks, soft spikes and a cap pulled low at a jaunty angle to help hide features from any CCTV. Wes knew where the cameras were and how to avoid any compromising footage. He sidled up to the driving range carrying a single pitching iron and a small bucket of balls. When the time was right he took an open tee box beside the Judge and began to hit balls. As the Judge placed a few clubs on the stand, he turned away and contorted his body, limbering up as usual for a minute or two before hitting from his own bucket. In a split second Wes quietly slipped a ball from his pocket and eased it among those in the Judge's bucket. He then casually hit one last ball and strode away. A minute later he was in his RV slowly exiting the parking lot when the explosion rocked the back of the clubhouse. The golf ball was a low level explosive made of black powder, fuel and oxidizer which would deflagrate, causing maximum damage in a confined area. Wes did not want any innocents to be injured, so this method insured that anybody outside of the 15' radius of the Judge's teeing area would have temporary hearing loss at worst. The Judge, on the other hand, would never try a case again, would never grant an early release to a convicted felon, would not even savor a gin-soaked olive floating in a martini. He would spend his last days sitting in a chair, staring at the wall with spittle dripping down his chin.

With the appetizer out of the way, Wes was now ready for the main course...... the killer. Steven Kadell lived barely twenty minutes from the country club, but much more caution was needed in a residential area, as a large RV cruising through the neighborhood and parked along a curb for any length of time was sure to draw attention. Walmart was the answer. Wes had scouted one within about two miles of the Kadell home on an earlier trip and calmly pulled into the rear of the parking lot. He untied his Trek hybrid bicycle from the back of the vehicle, strapped on his helmet and his backpack, donned his dark sunglasses and rode into the neighborhood where the Kadells lived. Again, he had done his homework and was intimately familiar with the streets and with the location of the house in question. He also knew that the Kadell family went to the 10:30 mass each Sunday; all of them that is except Steven who was shackled with an ankle bracelet and figuratively shackled with the shame of his sin. The less he was seen in public, the better for all. Once the family packed into the car and headed to church, Wes rode his bicycle into the recess of the cul-de-sac where the home stood beside a slight wooded ravine. He took refuge behind a large pin oak. He removed his backpack and from it he extracted a lightweight VR3 Tactical Drone with gesture recognition features and an altitude hold option to lock in height and location. He gently attached an explosive on the underside of the drone and remotely navigated it across the span of about 75 yards that separated him from the front of the Kadell home. Once it was locked in place and hovering at 10′, he activated the horn which was just loud enough to attract the attention of anyone in the house. Steven stepped outside on his porch and curiously walked out to investigate. Once he was in range, Wes activated the detonator button and the entire drone became a fiery explosive ball, sending hundreds of tiny shards of metal in a downward thrust and obliterating everything within a 30′ radius. Satisfied to have witnessed the killer get his due, Wes calmly walked his bicycle along to the back of the ravine, staying out of sight, and mounted it again when he reached an access road adjacent to the neighborhood. He quietly pedaled his way back to his RV, exited the parking lot, and continued west. He switched on a local news channel and waited for word of any breaking news about the days' events. He did not have to wait too long.

CHAPTER 3

EASTERN KENTUCKY

WES OFTEN WONDERED how he would feel once he had completed his missions that day. Despite a career of investigating killings, he himself had never intentionally wounded or killed anyone before and it was a strange sensation. He found his anger and hatred had easily given way to a sense of euphoria in the name of justice. He had planned these two events with the greatest details in mind and had left no trace of his presence. Law enforcement would be unlikely to be able to trace the purchase of the drone, which was in a thousand minute pieces. The exploding golf ball would likewise yield no clues. His years as a homicide investigator had taught him many tricks and were now serving him well.

The lush fabric of the Ohio Valley landscape spread wide and welcoming to Wes as he drove further into Kentucky, and soon the gentle valley gave way to rugged mountains dissected by streams and gradually to the rolling hills of the Mississippi Plateau to the south and a chain of low, steep hills directly ahead called The Knobs. There are many tough places to live in the U. S.; the ghost towns of Detroit, Gary and Camden for example, but the persistent poverty which plagues the Appalachias of eastern Kentucky just might make it the hardest place in the nation to live. The basic metrics used to define quality living such as education, household income, jobless rate, life expectancy and obesity, show the counties of Kentucky Coal Country among the bottom ten in the nation. Clay County was dead last with only 7.5% of its population having achieved a Bachelor's Degree, an unemployment rate of over 13%, and more than half of Clay County was rated in the obese category.

Wes had secured RV lodging in a park on the perimeter of Louisville for the night. Despite it being a mid-Sunday afternoon, traffic had slowed to nearly a crawl as he neared the I-265 beltway around the southeastern expanse of the city. His thoughts were interrupted by a breaking news report on the radio. Both "bombings" were being reported in Florence, Ky. and already local police officials were trying to tie the two together due to proximity, timing and methodology. This was as expected and Wes allowed himself a wry smile and thought "this is just the beginning friends".

It was a grisly scene at 5842 Farmingham Lane later that Sunday morning. A barrage of police cruisers, emergency medical vehicles and a fire truck converged on the scene within minutes after receiving a 911 call from a neighbor. Lights were flashing, crime scene tape was being put up and law enforcement had cordoned off the entire end of the block to protect the crime scene and obstruct the curious from nosing in. The district's Medical Examiner was already on site with two crime specialists who were taking photographs while detectives canvassed the neighbors for eye witnesses. Only one person, a middle aged woman who lived at the other end of the block, reported seeing a man riding a bicycle down the street earlier that morning. However she could confirm nothing more than dark clothes, a dark hat pulled low and she was not even sure enough to venture what race he was or what age, although she did describe him of being medium build. She had been out watering her hedge and noted him out of the corner of her eye. She thought nothing more of it until she realized that she never saw him come back out of the cul-de-sac, but assumed he was visiting a neighbor.

Betty Kadell and her children, Kayla and Lance, had a Sunday morning ritual. If the kids behaved in church they would stop by Krispy Kreme on the way home and choose whatever kind of doughnut they wanted. They also got a tart loaded with whipped cream for Dad as they knew it was his favorite. When their car turned on to Farmingham the sight in front of their house nearly sent Betty into shock. She pulled the car over to the curb and put it in park as a wave of nausea swept over her. She sat frozen for nearly a minute, torn between revulsion and curiousity. The kids pleading from the back seat interrupted her and she quickly shut the car off and admonished them to be quiet. She commanded them to stay put for a moment and slowly exited the car. Karen Cropper had been standing with the rest of the horrified onlookers when she turned and recognized Betty's car pull off to the side of the street. She slowly walked towards her trying to figure out what to say. She reached Betty as she was walking away from her car, saw the haunted look in her eyes and gave her a big hug. She did not let go of the embrace as both women sobbed, despite not being certain what the details were. "Honey, the kids don't need to see this. Why don't you all come to my house until this all gets sorted out. I'm sure the police will want to talk with us later." Betty went through the motions of retrieving the children and following Karen to her home in a zombie-like state, unable to think or even speak.

Ruth Kramer lived on the sixth floor of the Towering Oaks Condominiums. The condos sat immediately across the street from Florence Country Club, or more specifically across from the driving range. Towering Oaks in fact had no oaks that towered over the units at all. It had the requisite number of modest trees and low level shrubs dotting its landscape in order to gain approval for a permit from the county building commission, but not much more. It was an ambitious name and little more than a marketing ploy to try and put some grandiose twist to an otherwise unremarkable piece of land. Ruth was a life time smoker. She had picked up the nasty habit as a teen like so many others in this area of the country. Her husband Ray banished her to the outdoor patio whenever she needed a smoke - which was way too often for Ray. "If you're going to kill yourself, do it outside" he would say. And so it was that Ruth often sat for long stretches in her chair on the patio, nursing her habit and looking over the driving range watching all manners of golfers flail away at their sport. Though not a golfer herself, she had spent enough hours in observation of the range to recognize the regulars by their swings. Florence was not a large enough metropolis to sustain a first tier private country club, so Florence Country Club was semi-private, which allowed for unescorted guests to play golf there. Ruth had been a patio sitter long enough to not only recognize most of the regular members from her perch but even most of those guests who practiced on the range with any frequency. Therefore she was only mildly interested that Sunday morning as she drew heavily on her Marlboro to see a man whom she had never seen before stride up to the range. That fact alone would not have caught her attention, but to see him stroll out to the teeing area with only a single club in hand, hit no more than 2 or 3 balls, and then leave was pretty unusual. Still she thought little of it until the explosion occurred. The carnage was gut wrenching and Ruth watched in horror as Judge Brammer writhed on the ground in agony and numerous other golfers lay splayed out on the ground in shock. Ray rushed out to see what the noise was and looked to his wife for answers. She took a moment to compose herself and then told him what she had witnessed and wondered if it was coincidence that a stranger, armed with only a single club, hit a few balls and then left almost immediately before the explosion. They went down to see if they could help any of the victims and awaited the police investigators so that they could share Ruth's story. The crime scene at the country club was very much like that on Farmingham Lane. Once all the victims had been ambulanced away and the scene was combed for clues, the investigators sought out eye witnesses. Ruth and a handful of others were able to say with some degree of certainty that a caucasian male of medium build and middle age had been standing next to the judge for a very brief time minutes before the explosion. Nobody remembered ever seeing the man before, nobody had paid him much attention, and even Ruth had been too far away to see his face.

CHAPTER 4

FLORENCE, KY.

DETECTIVE BRENDAN DUGAN was packing the last of his items in his luggage in anticipation of his vacation beginning tomorrow morning. He had been planning a fly fishing trip to Montana for nearly a year and he could hardly contain his enthusiasm. His 6:30 a.m. Monday flight would take him directly into Bozeman and from there he would pick up his rental jeep and drive two hours into the interior of the Beartooth Mountains and to his lodging on the Madison River. The cutthroat trout were running and he couldn't wait to wet his line and to get far away from phones and the human population with all of its sordid problems for a week. HIs cell phone rang as he swung his well worn suitcase off the bed. He was tempted not to answer it but saw that it was Commissioner Williams. He swallowed hard, crossed his fingers and did his best to answer with a perky "Commissioner, I was just heading out the door on my vacation". "Cancel it" he heard on the other end of the phone. "We have a problem - a big one. One dead, one critical, and that one is a Circuit Court Judge with a national presence. There could be a connection between the two". "Commissioner, with all due respect" pleaded Dugan, but the line went dead. He just stared at the ceiling and shook his head.

Detective Dugan was on the scene at the country club within the hour. As the Metro's Chief Crime Investigator he was granted quick access and wasted no time in catching up with all police and medical responders on their findings. He scanned the notes taken from all of the witnesses and recognized that they had very little to go on other than a male suspect of perhaps middle age and of medium build. The make and source of the explosive would not be determined until forensics completed its lab analysis. However the fact that two similarly confined explosives were used that same morning and in that same town was too much for coincidence. His office had filled him in on the victim in the second bombing and his connection to the Judge on his way to the club. The prospect of a potential serial killer playing a vigilante role chilled him to the bones and he needed some answers, quickly. After getting clearance from his boss, he called the FBI headquarters in Washington, D.C. and asked to be patched through to its Behavioral Analysis Unit. A receptionist answered and Dugan left a message for Mark Raymond. Dugan knew Raymond casually; they had worked a case together a few years ago and Officer Dugan felt that he was one of the brightest minds he had ever met.

You can say what you want about the FBI, and after some very suspect leadership over the past several years anyone would be justified in being a skeptic. But Dugan knew that no organization can put together a team of crack investigators and get them into the field faster than the FBI. Despite it being Sunday afternoon, Officer Dugan received a call back from

Investigator Raymond within a half hour. After a quick exchange of pleasantries, Dugan laid out the two crime scenes for Raymond and his concern that someone trained with explosives and proven almost ghostlike in his execution could be playing vigilante. Raymond agreed and promised to have a team in place by morning.

CHAPTER 5

LOUISVILLE, KY.

WES WAS RELIEVED to put some distance between himself and Florence but continued to follow the news updates on the radio as he drove to Creekside RV Park just on the outskirts of the trendy Louisville suburb of Crescent Hill. It was one of the city's most desirable neighborhoods and a destination for young professionals and major league athletes. Notably, it was where DeMarcus Bogues lived after a fairly brief stint as a professional basketball player. DeMarcus had starred at the University of Kentucky for two seasons before flashing gifted athletic skills that made him a lottery pick in the NBA draft. He signed a huge five year contract with the Cleveland Cavaliers and played out that term before finally falling out of favor because of a poor work ethic and therefore not meeting the lofty expectations of a first round pick. More importantly, Bogues' contract was not renewed because of a trail of sexual allegations from 9 different women over his last few years on the team and it had caused bad press for the team and for the league. One of the alleged victims even committed suicide, noting in a letter by her body that she could no longer stand the scrutiny. All charges went to trial but none had enough evidence to convict Mr. Bogues who claimed that it was consensual in every case and that the women were just after his money and celebrity status. He had hired a very slimy high profile liberal attorney out of Chicago who got him off with community service and probation.

Wes piloted his RV into his reserved spot at Creekside RV resort, a fairly secluded spot with no other camper nearby. He hooked up his electrical power, leveled the coach and relaxed to enjoy a nice glass of red wine and a bowl of pasta that he hastily threw together. The sauce was out of a jar but as he warmed it and boiled some noodles he was just enough of a culinarian geek to add some toppings and give his meal a little pizazz. He methodically ate, drank his glass of a nice red blend wine and waited for the approach of dusk. Once again he slipped into his dark jeans, his dark sweat shirt, pulled his black ballcap low on his head and donned his backpack. He unlatched his Trek hybrid bicycle from the back of the RV and quietly made his way from the campsite to Windsor Park Estates, barely 3 miles away. It was completely dark when Wes arrived at Mr. Bogues 3 acre homestead, neatly separated from the other properties and with a minimum of security. Crouching in the dark behind a stand of maples and boxwoods in a natural area, Wes extracted his latest toy from his backpack - a four power Leopold infrared monocular that made anything with a heat signature show up in shades of yellow, orange and red. He had the device aimed across the yard at the front of the 4000 sq. ft. home set in the middle of the 3 acres. Wes had downloaded the layout of the house on his phone but had already committed to memory the blueprint and a real estate agent's video tour of the house. He could walk the place blindfolded, he thought, and not bump into a chair. Wes laid there and monitored activity for the next two hours until all action ceased. It was apparent that nobody was in the house with Mr. Bogues. It was midnight and Wes waited another hour during which he had seen no movement. Raising his monocular again he followed his planned route to avoid any motion sensing cameras and reached the junction box on the west wall where he disabled the cameras and overrode the security system. Checking once again to confirm there was no movement in the house, Wes worked his magic on the front lock and was inside in less than two minutes. He stepped across the carpeted foyer and tip-toed up the staircase to the master bedroom. He pressed his ear against the door and heard a muffled snoring. He quietly eased the door open and spotted the figure lying in the middle of the bed. He withdrew his .32 caliber beretta with suppressor and approached the sleeping figure. When he was beside the bed he pulled out his high beam halogen flashlight, aimed it at the lump and shook it. Bogues sat up with a start but was blinded by the glare of the flashlight. Wes, having assured himself that this was indeed his target, calmly said "Mr. Bogues, this one is for the ladies" and quickly fired two suppressed rounds into his head. On his way out, Wes wiped the doorknobs, the staircase railing and the junction box and calmly rode his bike back to his campsite. It would be late on Monday before anybody would note the absence of Mr. DeMarcus Bogues, and by that time Wes would be well on his way to Chicago. He nestled in under his blanket and slept peacefully with no stain of conscience.

CHAPTER 6

CHICAGO

THE DRIVE from Louisville to Chicago was due north for nearly 300 miles and Wes had allowed himself five hours for the trip. Along the way he rehearsed his next move to the finest detail. The two weekend trips that he had taken over the last several months had been specifically for this reason. He had identified several high profile cases of "perps" who had gotten off easy and liberal criminal defense lawyers and judges who were instrumental in facilitating that. Trial lawyers are most often more liberal than the rest of the population. And they overwhelmingly contribute to the local Democratic candidates and to the National Democratic Party; and nowhere more than in Chicago. Rafael Ovechkin was no exception. He was a managing partner with the prestigious law firm of King & McKenzie. Rankings from Vault's Annual Associates Survey for 2021 had King & McKenzie near the top of the list for criminal defense lawyers. A study entitled "Lawyers lean to the left" also had the firm as among the most liberal in the city. Rafael was also a heavy contributor to the Democratic Party and his tentacles reached deeply into city politics. It was Ovechkin who allowed that scumbag rapist Bogues to walk and Wes would seek justice on behalf of the women.

King & McKenzie's offices were perched on the prestigious "Miracle Mile", a 13-block stretch along Michigan Avenue. It's a spectacular run of restaurants, skyscrapers, museums and hotels and includes the 1451' Willis Tower (formerly the Sears Tower). Within the shadow of the Willis Tower stood the King & McKenzie law offices. This is where Mr. Ovechkin plied his trade from his spacious office on the seventh floor. On his earlier trip, Wes had leisurely dined for several hours on the outdoor terrace of Banderas Restaurant, just across the street from the offices. On that trip he had studied a local newspaper, a map of the downtown area and a tourist guide; all the while watching traffic patterns, people, identifying CCTV cameras and figuring out how best to blend in with the local populace. Today he was again at Banderas late in the afternoon seated in the second row of tables on the patio and enjoying its signature Macho Salad. He had finished his meal and was nursing his third glass of soda water when at about 5:30 the staff from King & McKenzie began exiting the front door. He watched closely and had a photo of Ovechkin clutched closely on his phone. He had an excellent view but saw no sign of the sleazy lawyer. He decided to have a little fun at Ovechkin's expense, knowing that he would likely have heard by now about the murder of his former client, DeMarcus Bogues. He thumbed the screen on his burn phone and connected to the internet via a VPN. He then called up WhatsApp and scrolled until he had the name of Rafael Ovechkin in front of him. He opened his note-taking app, read the note again that he had drafted earlier in the day, and sent it. Twenty minutes later the portly Mr. Ovechkin exited the main entrance of the offices looking nervously around. There was no mistaking the man. It was a florid, jowly face with a ruddy complexion and a Vitalis combover that Wes watched ponderously waddle to the car park. His shirt collar was open and he was noticeably sweating. Wes called for his bill, paid it along with a generous tip for occupying the table beyond normal meal limits and headed for where he had chained his bike within sight of the reserved parking lot where he had made a quick visit before going to the restaurant. As he straddled his Trek for his journey back to the campsite he heard a loud explosion and saw evidence of the same emanating from the parking spot where Mr. Rafael Ovechkin had parked his Mercdes under his name stenciled on the wall. One of humanity's least desirable people ceased to exist.

CHAPTER 7

MONDAY

WES' ride back to the RV park was uneventful. He had avoided any curious eyes as he casually pedaled away from the crime scene. Just another nondescript guy on a bike, masked and dressed in black. Four targets, he thought, four successes, and he was certain that law enforcement officials in Florence, Louisville, and now Chicago would be extremely frustrated with a lack of any witnesses or tangible clues. His plan was working to perfection. He had created the personna of a ghost-like specter, skilled with explosives, enacting revenge on crooks and their cronies and leaving no trail. As time went by he suspected that as each subsequent killing was catalogued and the victims linked to criminal enterprise, it would be hard for the casual citizen to condemn these actions. Red blooded, law abiding Americans had seen enough over the last few years and might even begin to cheer on this vigilante. For the time being however he knew it was time to lay low, let things simmer just a little and see how law enforcement was progressing with this mystery. Thus far it had publicly asked for help from the public if anyone had any information. That in itself was a sign that they were desperate and clueless.

Wes returned to his camper, opened a cold beer, enjoyed the chill as it hit his tongue and the back of his throat, and flipped open his laptop to watch for breaking news. At this time of year the campsite was referred to as a "dry site", meaning no water or sewer was supplied to campers; only electricity. His RV had a "black tank" which would handle his sewage for a week and enough fresh water to see him through that time. Being a dry campsite meant less people and that was just fine for Wes who effectively had his area of the resort to himself. Dinner was a ground turkey meatloaf that he had assembled and had tossed in the oven. As he reached for a second beer his laptop lit up with the lead story of a car bombing in the downtown area. The victim was not identified, pending notifying next of kin, but a middle-aged male was confirmed dead and the term "domestic terrorism" was heard for the first time and potentially linked to three similar explosions in the last day and a half across the upper mideast corridor of the U.S. Wes ceremoniously closed his laptop, resumed drinking his beer with smug satisfaction, and nuked some Quinoa while his meatloaf finished cooking.

Move over New York because Chicago, "the Second City", had overtaken the Big Apple in recent years and had achieved the dubious distinction of being labeled the murder capital of the U.S. More than 500 murders were logged in the city every year, with most of them going unsolved. This was not surprising considering that the bulk of these occurred on the gang infested south side of Chicago where groups like the Bloods, the Crips the Latin Kings and the Gangster Disciples all ruled their turf without fear of police reprisal. The inept city government was complicit in this as it had defunded the police effort across the city, only further emboldening the gangs around the neighborhoods of Riverdale, Englewood, Washington Park and, worst of all, West Garfield Park. The neighborhoods were tough and dileneated by ethnicity and gang colors. The Hispanics had become the largest gang over the past few decades and preferred yellow and gold colors to identify their allegiance. The Blacks stuck with their black colors and hoodies to match while MS 13 favored blue. The most fearsome gang was the Referees which sported a combination of black & blue. When any of them performed a "hit", they blew a whistle and held up a red card indicating that their mission was accomplished. Curiously, all of these gangs had only recently returned to sporting their gang colors. Until the defunding police effort eased patrols, gangs were reluctant to flaunt their colors for fear of calling unwanted police attention to themselves. Now they resumed that practice with the vigor of the gangs in the 80s & 90s - and were proud to identify with their brethren. The turf wars were an absolute bloodletting with no regard at all for local law enforcement. What sane policeman would ever willingly agree to a beat on the southside of Chicago?

Chicago's Transit Authority's train system, known as the "EL", shortened for elevated, emanated from downtown across the breadth of the city in all directions and served 140 stations. It was a convenient way to get anywhere that one wanted but unfortunately it too had the reputation of being unsafe. Particularly the Belmont Red Line, the Argle Red Line and the Washington Blue Line, all of which stretched out into the southside neighborhoods. The city had recently spent $26 million for a surveillance network of 3600 cameras on all trains and platforms which upgraded public safety on most lines but had minimal effect on the gang territories. All of this information had been a part of Wes' thorough review of the city of Chicago as he prepared to launch his most ambitious effort yet - beginning first thing in the morning.

CHAPTER 8

THE "EL"

WES ENJOYED A LIGHT, leisurely breakfast of bran flakes and a protein shake. As he savored the last of his second cup of coffee he studied his map of the CTA train system for the umpteenth time. The Red Line at Logan Park was within walking distance and a train was scheduled to come through every 12 minutes to pick up passengers. He stepped from his coach and breathed deeply of the crisp late fall air. From this vantage point on one of Chicago's westernmost surburbs he had a nice unobscured view of the impressive city skyline. He began the six block walk to Logan Station where he would hop the Red Line Loop through downtown and transfer to the Orange Line which would eventually carry him to the crime ridden southwest side. At 55 years of age, Wes was still pretty fit thanks to his common sense discipline. He was perhaps just a pound of two thicker than at his prime but he could hold his own with anyone his age after decades of police defensive training classes and his fitness routine.

Wes had "dressed down" to look like every other indistinguishable John Doe who rode the rails. A layer of loose clothing hid his light kevlar vest and the bulge of his beretta. As he hopped the "EL" the smell of urine was immediately evident and scraps of litter dotted the worn carpet. Wes was all too aware that many of the homeless often spent their nights on the train to stay warm and would often relieve themselves in place rather than disembark to meet Mother Nature's call. Eventually, either their urge for a drug fix or a need to find something to eat would drive them to leave the train car. His car this morning was very sparsely occupied; one or two urchins curled up asleep on seats, another one or two with hollowed eyes staring off into the universe and several bros with large headphones on completely absorbed in rap music that could be heard from the opposite end of the car. The rail operator for this car was a large minority female who more than filled her driver's seat at the front car and seemed oblivious to anything behind her. CTA rail operators often endured long hours, fatigue and boredom in their duties and it was not in their best interest to try and monitor passenger behavior. Train riders on this line were, by and large, a suspect and eclectic mix of people, and train operators focused mainly on getting to the next station without incident. The best that the three Chicago agencies which had responsibility for monitoring the rails could hope for was to recover at least 50% of their operating costs from fares. This was a constant challenge however and the remainder had to be subsidized by the city. "Jumpers" who leapt the turnstiles were essentially ignored for their low level crime. The irony of this was that these jumpers were allowed to operate with impunity but they were most often the same punks who pulled robberies on the "EL" or sexually molested passengers. You couldn't ignore one without feeling the impact of the other. Chicago crime was off the charts thought Wes and their ultra-liberal, radical and combative lesbian Mayor deflected all blame to police. They deserve what they get, thought Wes, if the voters chose to put this whacko in power.

He kept his hat pulled low and his mask on as he passed the time along his route, pretending to listen to tunes through his ear buds. No music was playing however, as he wanted his senses on high alert. When he finally stepped out of the car and onto the platform at West Garfield Park, he cautiously glanced left and right. He then crossed the tracks toward Halstead Street with head bowed low and shoulders slumped forward. He shuffled noncommittally through the warehouse district that included a crumbling infrastructure of factories, steel mills and meat plants. In its heyday at the turn of last century it had employed tens of thousands of immigrants, migrants and also those minorities who fled the racist south. These hearty souls were willing to work for substandard wages and live in tenement slums. He spent most of his day slinking through the alleyways and streets and by nightfall had gotten a pretty good lay of the area. The district sprawl reluctantly gave way to a few stumbling commercial enterprises. Dollar General stood on the opposite side of Halstead St. from an old meat plant. A pawn shop managed to scratch out a living on the same block, and further down a cash-n-carry grocery did a robust business in cigarettes, beer, munchies and rolling papers. Shop owners were caged behind bullet proof glass and most featured an alarm button poised within easy reach if they saw an undesirable assembly of hoodlums. The best the proprietor could hope for was some timely police response. It was here that Wes quietly lurked in the shadows and tried to anticipate where the mob might make its next move. It was evident where most of the smash and grab activities had taken place lately and a pattern seemed to be developing. Mob activities tracked towards the next outlying neighborhood where a few ambitious storefronts remained undamaged. There were plenty of lifeless souls wandering aimlessly on the streets late at night and drug trafficking was everywhere. By 3:00 a.m. Wes had seen all that he needed and retraced his route back to his RV. Over the next 3 nights he repeated these same measures, only expanding his surveillance a little more each night to see the movement of the mob and note its progress towards its next potential targets.

FOUR DAYS HAD PASSED since the sensational murder of sleazeball lawyer Rafael Ovechkin. The media fascination had subsided and news had moved from the front page of the Tribune to the latter pages of section B, providing only the most sketchy investigation updates - of which there were few. Wes was appreciative of the relative calm that ensued and was pleased that Chicago could resume its normal weekend activity of seeing only about 30 - 40 shootings in this city, a city which forebade the ownership of all guns for its citizens. Tonight's return to the southside for Wes would involve greater preparation and, unavoidably, slightly more risk. He would leave his compact beretta behind in favor of his Remington (CSR) concealable sniper rifle. A sweet little 7.62 mm bolt action suppressed sniper carbine with a 15″ removable carbon fiber barrel. He went to his bedroom, got on his knees and slid back a disguised panel under his bed to get the rucksack which housed this weapon. He also grabbed the 1.5 lb. aerosol cannister of Sarin Nerve Gas.

At about 2:00 that afternoon a non-descript figure of medium height and medium build, clothed in dark jeans, dark hoodie, a dark hat and with a mask on stepped from his RV into a relentless drizzle. He welcomed the rain as it would further cloak his movements tonight. He walked the 6 blocks to Logan Park and hopped the red line for the fourth and final time. Again his destination tonight was West Garfield Park, arguably the toughest neighborhood in Chicago. He had learned through his reading this past week a brief history of the neighborhood. Now as he rode the rails he did a deeper internet dive on his burner phone to learn more. Prior to WWII, the neighborhood was home to Irish, German and Russian immigrants. In the 50s African Americans began moving in and realtors began panic peddling, scaring the whites out. In a matter of a decade West Garfield went from majority white to majority black and today was 93% black. It has seen some tough times. Fifty years ago riots devastated much of south Chicago after the Martin Luther King assassination. It slowly recovered over time but then after George Floyd's killing, the commercial district was vandalized and looted once again. Most businesses lost 75% of their income. However a resilient population worked with the Garfield Community Council to spur economic development with existing and potential businesses. At the crossroads of this old versus new was the 28th Ward, which still managed to stand in defiance of mob activity. Most of the business owners had been in the community for a long time and refused to give up. It was this stretch called the Madison Corridor where Wes was headed.

He stepped from the train platform into the shadows and waited for his eyes to adjust. As he walked along the now familiar route to the Corridor he assumed a posture that said "don't mess with me and I won't mess with you"; purposeful but not confrontational. Body language was important on the south side. After all, this was the home of Jim Croce's "Bad, bad Leroy Brown". There was still some daylight and the young toughs who would be lurking in the alleyways, getting high on weed and cheap wine, would not be around for a few hours yet. They had gathered here every night this week, Wes observed, but tonight was Friday and the throng seemed to be getting antsier each night. He identified an electronics store at the edge of the commercial district where he had chosen to hang his cannister of Sarin. He suspended it from the bottom of a fire escape at a height of about 10' in the alleyway at the corner where the thugs had gathered each previous evening of his visits. He moved across the street to an abandoned building and set up camp. He assembled his rifle, sighted on the aerosol cannister and when the red laser beam found its target he settled back and waited for nightfall.

As darkness descended the unruly mob numbers grew and by nine p.m. there appeared to be at least 40 of them. The air hung heavy with the smell of marijuana and the noise level gradually rose as the alcohol assumed control of emotions. Before long Wes could see that the mob was itchy and looking for trouble. The barred windowfront taunted them with the newest electronic gadgetry. It was only a matter of time before the first of them threw a brick through the window. Others tried to kick in the front door, cheered on by the remaining hooligans. Wes slowly raised his rifle and at the height of the insanity he calmly fired a round into the cannister which imme- diatley exploded, releasing the dangerous nerve agent. The area of impact was about a 50 meter radius and the Sarin, which was heavier than the air, quickly dispersed downward leaving almost nobody unaffected. There was a moment of eerie silence, then confusion, then the screams began. The nerve gas burns the eyes and skin almost immediately followed quickly by labored breathing as air passages become restricted. Wes calmly broke down his rifle, shouldered his rucksack and with loud cries and wails in his wake he unobtrusively made his way back across the tracks towards Halstead Street to the train station. He retraced his route back to his RV and well before midnight he was snug in his bed satisfied with his nights' work and plotting his next move. It was time to leave Chicago.

CHAPTER 10

CHI TOWN

LINCOLN PARK WAS one of Chicago's most desirable neighborhoods with its manicured lawns, Botanical Garden, the acclaimed Lincoln Park Zoo and beautiful homes along the lakefront trail leading to the Chicago River and Lake Michigan. Ray Walker had lived there most of his adult life and retired there after a successful career in stock trading. One of his few remaining daily pleasures was to rise early each morning, as so many of his age did, make a fresh pot of coffee, and retrieve the Chicago Tribune from his driveway no later than 6:00 a.m. He was definitely old school, a creature of habit, and made no apologies for it. He liked nothing more than having a steaming cup of coffee in hand and leafing through the local and national news each morning. As he trudged down his driveway in slippers and robe he again made a mental note to tip his paper carrier this coming Christmas season. It seemed that no matter how early he went out for the paper, it was always there. This morning however that was not to be the case. In fact it would be several more hours before Ray's paper would arrive. The events in West Garfield Park the previous night had stopped the presses in mid-print so that the Tribune could capture the breaking story of the nerve gas attack on its front page. When the Tribune did arrive the headline read **Domestic Terrorist Attack on Southside,** and the intervening pages gave the gruesome details of the crime scene and the updated number of injured and those in critical condition.

A dozen Federal FBI Agents were flown in early that next morning and set up a War Room in the conference space of a local southside police department. The Bureau agents were joined by assets from U.S. Customs, some Marshals Service Deputies and a couple of ATF guys who had been working a lower level counterfeit case in Kankakee, Illinois. White boards had been positioned up front in the room, a bank of satellite phones linked other intelligence agencies in and a video screen rolled continuous photos of last nights' crime scene. Makeshift tables and chairs dotted the room and agents were sipping coffee from styrofoam cups and poring over a smattering of documents. Lead Special FBI Investigator Mark Raymond had been rushed over from his ongoing investigation in Louisville. He called for attention in the room and once things quieted he introduced himself. He thanked the team members for their quick response and laid out his findings thus far based upon the Ohio & Kentucky bombings.

"Ladies and gentlemen, we have a dead convicted felon who was out on release, a nearly dead Circuit Court Judge who happened to grant his appeal, a former professional athlete shot in his bed and his criminal defense lawyer who spared his client a rape charge was blown up in his car. This all occurred in the span of a couple of days and similar explosives were used in three of the cases. A .32 caliber beretta was the weapon on the fourth. Then last night a canister of Sarin was detonated over a gang of toughs on the Southside and the injury count is climbing. What is the connection? Were there any witnesses? Do we have any credible leads? Was this the work of one person or several? Is there a discernible pattern here and, if so, where is the next likely target?" Agent Raymond paused for effect. "This much I can tell you, we are looking for a professional - of that I'm certain. I have been on site this week for the first four cases and we have very little to go on. The suspect is thought to be a white male of medium height and build, and no solid leads yet on his age. Thus far no trace on the weapon or the explosives. It seems our suspect is at least two steps ahead of us at every turn. In essence, we just don't have a lot to go on" The room remained quiet and Raymond took the opportunity to assign teams to the various tasks and then made his closing remarks. "I thank you for your commitment to this investigation and ask you to think about each of those questions I laid out for you. I remind you of our motto, FBI...........fidelity, bravery and integrity. Let's catch this bastard!"

CHAPTER 11

MINNEAPOLIS

WES AWOKE EARLY, swallowed a quick cup of coffee, then disconnected his power at the RV site and was on the road to Minneapolis before 7:00 a.m. Northbound traffic heading out of the city was a little light as he headed up Interstate 90. It was nearly a 400 mile trip and he expected an easy seven hour drive. As the sun rose over his right shoulder a bluebird clear sky to greeted him. His trip was uneventful though by the end of his journey that day winter weather had snarled the traffic heading into Minneapolis as the low setting sun beckoned him west from the horizon. Once again he had identified a "dry" campsite on the city outskirts and had reserved a spot for a couple of nights. It was a colder than normal November and the maples along the route had lost their leaves, turning them into dark and skeletal figures along the two lane road greeting him on his drive to the RV resort. This late in the year not many people headed to the great upper midwest on vacation. Technically, it was not really winter yet but Minnesota did not adhere to any calendar in meting out its weather. In fact his radio reported that the first major snowstorm of the year was headed across the upper U. S. Cold easterly wet winds swept off the Pacific Northwest coast and were dumping unprecedented amounts of snowfall across the Cascades and Rockies. It was a skier's delight but travelers, and especially those in oversized vehicles, had to be careful of icy roads. The weather report was interrupted by breaking news about the gas poisoning the previous night in a Chicago suburb. The media was hysterical and local and federal agencies were frantic for information. Conspiracy theories ran rampant but law enforcement had so little to work with and were reluctant to give out much information. Again, a central theme was slowly emerging through the public that the mastermind behind this was a champion for the little guy. If, in fact, all of these recent incidents were tied together, it was becoming evident that all of these victims were deserving and there wasn't much sympathy. "Brilliant", thought Wes to himself. His expectations had already been exceeded.

This was not an ideal time to visit good old "MinneS-NOWta" chuckled Wes to himself as he remembered the line from the TV weatherman of his childhood days. However stories of the summer riots and video clips of the culture clashes between Minnesota natives and the large communities of transplanted Somalis and Ethiopians around the city begged for his attention. He kept the needle just under 70 mph to remain off the radar and off the grid. Before he left on this trip he had removed the battery from his cellphone and had only used a burner phone once to do his internet search before quickly disposing of it in a fashion that would even put Hillary Clinton to shame. He pulled out a second burner phone and dialed a number in the toney Minneapolis neighborhood of Richfield.

Marcia Patterson was an old college friend. Her boyfriend at the time was Wes' best friend, so they had often hung out with Wes and his girlfriend. They remained Christmas card buddies over the years, especially after the tragic death of Marcia's husband several years ago. They had committed to catching up then for old times sake in the near future and this seemed like an ideal opportunity. Wes had been out of the social scene for some time now, considering himself single beyond repair, but he did want to keep his promise to Marcia and see how she was doing. Marcia was a dynamic, blond beauty and he had always enjoyed her company. It would be good to hear how things were going in her life and how she was coping with the loss of her husband. He dialed the burner phone and got Marcia's voicemail after the fourth ring. He left a message saying he would be in town and hoped to catch up for dinner while he was there.

Marcia had always looked ten years younger than her age, and her yoga regiment and prudent diet over the years were paying great dividends even now. She was in downtown Minneapolis doing some early Christmas shopping and looking resplendent walking the sidewalks in a pearl colored silk blouse with just a slightly provocative neckline, tight charcoal wool slacks and black leather high heeled boots that rode mid-calf. The ensemble was accented by a waist length rabbit fur jacket cinched tightly around her narrow waist. Her long blonde hair peeked out from under a saucy knitted woolen cap that matched her slacks. She was aware of the appreciative looks she was getting from men passing by. Seeing herself in the window reflection, she had to agree that the look was a good one. She had selected a small clutch that she easily carried in her right hand and when her cell phone rang she felt its vibration through the purse. She opted to let the caller leave a message so that she could continue her dash among the shops and duck out of the blustery winds that raced through the corridors between the downtown buildings.

CHAPTER 12

SATURDAY NIGHT

WES' guesstimate was not far off and in just under seven hours
he reached the outlying areas of the Twin Cities and used his
good old Rand McNally road map to navigate his way to Paul
Bunyan Park. He eschewed using his GPS, as once again he
preferred to not leave any electronic footprint. He had been in
law enforcement long enough and had seen enough tidbits of
the latest electronic surveillance equipment to understand
what the NSA and the other intelligences agencies were
capable of. It had been over ten years since Edward Snowden
had been taken down for blowing the whistle on government
surveilling. Snowden may have been labeled a traitor by some
but it was a great expose' of just how far reaching the government's technology was and how liberally it was being applied to
ordinary citizens. It was mid-afternoon and a blustery 37
degrees when he checked in. He paid cash and drove to his
campsite where he quickly hooked up his power and cranked
on the heat. He was not at all surprised that he was one of just a
few other travelers scattered across the park. He poured
himself three generous fingers of his favorite Woodford Reserve

Bourbon in a rocks glass, dropped in a couple of ice cubes, and stirred in a splash of bottled water. He settled back in supreme comfort and allowed the evening to unfold.

Marcia returned to her condo in Richfield late that afternoon. She unloaded her bags and kicked off her boots to massage her feet. Those cowgirl kickers may look pretty damned sexy, she thought, but when you've had your feet tucked in them all day you eventually have to pay the devil his due. She settled on her couch with her legs stretched horizontally across the cushions. She bent at the waist, reached out and grabbed her toes and held the position for a minute to stretch the hamstrings. A moment later she pulled out her cell phone to check for messages. Her phone had only rung once while she was out and she did not recognize the number so she listened to the message. She was tingling with excitement when she heard Wes' voice. It had been several years since the death of her husband and she had withdrawn to her inner self to combat the grief. She buried herself in her work and her workouts knowing that at some point she would eventually need to rejoin society. Wes was a dear friend and had been there for Frank's funeral and for emotional support. He had randomly kept in touch to make sure she was okay and it would be good to see him again and perhaps start to put the pieces of her social life back together. A dinner with an old friend might be a good first step. She nervously dialed the number and waited for Wes to answer. Her heart was fluttering like a school girl about to go out on her first date. "Thank you for returning my call" she heard from the other end. "Well of course" she said, "it is so good to hear your voice. When did you get into town? How long are you here for? How long do you plan on staying?" "Wait, wait" said Wes, "that's a lot of questions and it sounds to me like we better tackle all of those over dinner, and catch up on what you have been doing. Are you free tonight?" "Yes I am and I would love to see you. Just tell me when and where" said Marcia, wondering if that was a little too forward. "Well" said Wes, "there's the rub. I am actually in my RV at Paul Bunyan Park about 20 minutes south of you. The problem is that I don't have a car and navigating this monster through the weather and city traffic at night can get a little sticky". "Perfect" she said, I know just the right restaurant in Bloomington, halfway between you and I; The Urban Table. It has a 'to die for' lamb pie. Sit tight and I'll be there in half an hour, I know where the park is so be looking for me. Dress casually and bring your appetite". "You're on" smiled Wes, "see you then" and he hung up in anticipation of a great night out to take his mind off of his deeds of the past week.

CHAPTER 13

THE URBAN TABLE

WES HAD BEEN WATCHING out the window and soon noted a pair of headlights appear and slowly roll through the camping area. He exited the steps and waved as a dark, late model Buick Regal rolled up to his coach. One long and shapely leg stretched out of the car door followed by the other and Wes caught his breath as Marcia gracefully exited the car. Her skirt had hiked to mid-thigh exposing a pair of toned and alluring legs. She warmly embraced him and he returned the embrace with equal intensity and let it linger. No words were needed at that moment, the hug was long and spoke volumes. "You look fantastic", he finally managed once they surrendered their hold. "Thank you", she blushed, "and look at you, a guy in his mid-50's who still has a head full of hair and is not toting around a paunch. You look like you haven't gained an ounce since our days at St. Olaf's College. And look at this mobile home will you?". "RV" Wes corrected her, "there's a difference and I'll give you the nickel tour later but what do you say we go eat, I'm starving". "Absolutely, but I'm buying. You are in my town now, you left years ago. Besides you're my guest and they know me at The Urban Table so we'll get a little extra coddling if I pay". "Okay, no argument, but I've got the next one, now let's get in your warm car and you can tell me all about what you've been doing on the way over".

It was only a ten minute drive to the restaurant and Marcia and Wes used every second of it filling each other in on their lives. She told him how she was managing to cope with Franks' death after two muggers brutally beat him on a downtown street in Minneapolis, stole his wallet and jewelry and were never apprehended as the crime got lost in the myriad of so many others on the violent Minneapolis city streets these days. "Just another statistic" she said, "so I've lost myself in my work as a clothes buyer for a major department chain and I work out all my frustration as a Yoga Instructor three nights a week. The city is not the same as when we went to school here Wes. Since Obama relocated those huge communities of Somalis and Sudanese on the north side, the culture clash has been horrific. And I don't necessarily blame them. They were liberated from the oppression of their homelands only to be inserted into a totally unfamiliar country that is on the other side of the equator. It is completely foreign to them and frankly not particularly welcoming either. It has changed all of our lives and there is a very uneasy tolerance which you just have to believe could erupt at any time. It's a boiling kettle. And to make matters even worse", she continued, "the Minneapolis City Council just recently approved broadcasting the Muslim call to prayer five times a day across the city. The first is at sunrise, the last at sunset, with the others interspersed, so your life is interrupted five times a day, every day. You walk the streets around here and see what's going on and don't know if you're in St. Paul or Baghdad. This city has been in decline for decades as the Democrats pushed their giveaway programs which led to the inner city slowly rotting. And then once Obama relocated the hordes of Somalis here it sent us over the edge. The tenement slums are out of control and downtown Minneapolis is following the pattern of decay that plagues Detroit. Is this what freedom of religion was supposed to bring us?. I think not." She took a deep breath, realizing at that moment that it was the first time she had unloaded her frustrations like this on anyone - much less an old friend. "I'm so sorry", she said.

Wes had listened without saying a word and when Marcia relaxed he then told her about his career with the Criminal Investigation Division in the U.S. Army after getting his degree in criminal justice. He said he enjoyed many of the challenges of his occupation but the long hours cost him his marriage and between that and all the red tape of the bureaucracy these days he had finally burnt out. "I'm a liberated man now Marcia but I'm not sure what I've been liberated for. It's all still so new and my only interest for the moment is to decompress, get away and sort things out for the final chapter of my life. I have 'gone off the grid' for a while, as they say, so in that regard we still have a lot in common as we both search for a new purpose in the world that is left to us."

The Urban Table was hopping for a week night. Marcia claimed one of the last parking spaces and the two of them quickly headed inside to get out of the cold. Wes' mouth begin to water the moment they stepped from the cold and into the richly decorated restaurant where a deluge of aromas awaited him. He was further warmed by Marcia's hand leading him to meet Jean Francois who greeted her at the podium and scolded her for waiting this long to return. She accepted the good natured chastising and a peck on the cheek, and then intro-duced Wes as an old college friend from St. Olaf's. "Oui

Madam, I am familiar with St. Olaf's and in fact teach French classes there two nights a week to you Yankees", he smiled. "We have a small waiting list but let me escort you to a seat at the bar and I will retrieve you when a table opens up". He led them to the only two empty bar stools and excused himself. Wes helped Marcia remove her coat before they sat down and the effect was breathtaking. She wore black stilletos and a black form fitting dress with a slit up to mid thigh. "Jesus Marcia, you've been taking care of yourself. Talk about someone who hasn't gained an ounce since college! You've just readjusted it to all the right places". "Stop it", she said but she couldn't hide the pleasure of a good old fashioned compliment from an attractive man. They ordered drinks and soaked in the atmosphere of the place while they continued to share their stories. It was already proving to be a very special evening out but, unfortunately, was soon interrupted by a buzz across the room. The couple swung around on their barstools and saw Congresswoman Ilhan Omar at the podium with her husband on her arm, her third in the last four years. Her entourage of security personnel and the usual hangers-on followed closely behind. A fuss was made over finding an available table and soon Jean Francois artfully shifted a few chairs and whispered in a few ears and a table for eight was freed up on the back wall in full sight of the other tables. Its flanks were protected by a couple of pit bulls with shaved heads and noticeable bulges just above their beltlines.

"Do you know who that is" asked Marcia. "No, said Wes and based upon what I'm seeing I'm not sure that I want to". "That is Ilhan Omar and I'm not sure that two security thugs are enough. She is reviled here for her radical politics and if it weren't for that large invasion of refugees to our city she would never have had a chance to be elected. Yet here she is brazenly jumping the reservation list and leaving us the indignation to have to accept it. I'm sorry Wes, but all of a sudden I have lost my appetite. Would you mind if we left?". "Of course" he said, "we can go back to the RV, pop some corn and uncork a bottle of chardonnay". "You sure know how to charm a girl - that sounds wonderful, anything but staying here and having to look at her all night". They paid their bar tab, Wes regretfully helped Marcia cover up with her coat and they made their apologies to Jean Francois on the way out the door. Wes wanted to swing by the Omar table on his way out and suggest that they try the camel toe special tonight but thought better of it. No need to call attention to himself under the circumstances.

CHAPTER 14

THE TWIN CITIES

THE DRIVE back to the campsite was a little more somber than the trip to the restaurant. Both Marcia and Wes tried to shake off their distaste for Omar and her cronies. By the time they reached the RV they had managed to put it out of their mind and focus on other things. Wes opened the 'fridge and pulled out a bottle of Cupcake Chardonnay while he handed Marcia a bag of light butter popcorn to slip into the microwave. With those tasks complete they settled into the couch, clinked their glasses and shared the popcorn out of the same bowl. It felt so natural for these long-time friends to sit close together with stockinged feet on the coffee table and continue to fill in the gaps since they had seen each other. Once they exhausted the most immediate topics, Wes picked up the remote and flipped on the 11:00 news to see if the world was still out there. The weather forecaster was predicting temps in the teens tonight and the possibility of snow tomorrow. That brought a chill to Marcia. "Wes, I don't want to go home tonight" she coyly pleaded. "It is so miserable out there and I feel so good in your company here". Wes' heart leaped. He broke into the tune

"Baby it's cold outside", for which he received a good natured punch. "Baby you'll freeze out there - it's up to your knees out there" he lyrically sang, and received another punch. "Well one thing for sure" said Marcia, "is that you haven't taken any voice lessons in the years since I've seen you". "No' he playfully answered but I have taken etiquette classes and what gentleman could turn a lovely lady out into the cold on a night like this? Of course you can stay. I'll give you my room and this couch pulls out to a sleeper. I make a mean cup of coffee in the morning as well". He hopped up to refill their glasses and threw a comforter over them both.

The two continued to snuggle deeper under the blanket and hold each other until the volume raised just a notch on the TV as the late breaking news caught their attention. A reporter was holding a microphone in front of a large man who was identified as FBI Special Investigative Agent Mark Raymond. The backdrop was obviously the crime scene of note and four agents in hazmat suits appeared to be sifting the carnage. Agent Raymond was about to give an update. In a voice that sounded like gravel sliding off a shovel he said that he had assembled a task force of high ranking agents from every law enforcement agency under the DOJ umbrella and was calling for a nation-wide manhunt for one or more domestic terrorists. He continued that he had a probe in progress of five different crime scenes, from Ohio to Kentucky to Chicago. All scenes had been photographed and processed but the names of the latest victims had not yet been released. Agent Raymond confirmed that there were more than 30 victims thus far and that every indica-tion pointed to the crimes being linked. The reporter pressed for more information but Raymond was resolute that he had no more to offer at this time. Marcia had gotten very quiet and Wes looked over to see her teary-eyed. He hugged her even more tightly and assured her that she had nothing to worry about. "You don't understand", she said. "From what I've seen and read, these were all bad people and somebody is finally exacting justice. My husbands' killers are still out there and I would love to see them get their due." Wes warmed even further with the idea that Marcia might actually condone his recent actions, but he remained quiet and held her tightly until they both drifted off into a comfortable sleep.

CHAPTER 15

PAUL BUNYAN PARK

WES WAS the first to awake early the next morning. He opened his eyes and slowly regained his senses. What a delightful night that was, he thought. He hadn't had those sensations stirred within in him in years. He wasn't able to see the clock from where he lay but he could see that it was still dark outside. Beside him lay Marcia in all of her angelic inno- cence; her long blonde hair lightly tousled and framing her pretty face. Her head still rested on his shoulder. He moved as quietly as he could, uncovered, and tip-toed his way to the kitchen to put on a pot of coffee. While the coffee brewed, he went to his wardrobe and pulled an old flannel shirt off the hanger. He returned to the couch and placed it beside Marcia. With the coffee in full brew mode and the aromas wafting through the cabin, Marcia slowly began to stir. "Good Morning" she said in a sleepy voice, "I haven't slept that well in years". "I was thinking the same thing", said Wes, maybe we should do that more often". "Oh you naughty boy", she countered, is that an offer?". He smiled, walked over to her and placed the flannel shirt beside her. "It sure beats sleeping pills. Why don't you take this shirt, go freshen up in the bathroom and get out of those clothes. I'll have the coffee waiting by the time you get back". He could not keep himself from glancing after her as she retreated down the hallway to the bathroom.

By the time Marcia returned, her hair was loosely brushed into place and she looked adorable with the flannel shirt hitting just above her kneecaps and her socks flopping loosely around her ankles. She beamed a smile of perfect white teeth at Wes and confessed to using his toothbrush and toothpaste to rid herself of morning mouth. "You did me a favor", he said. "I would hate to have to share breakfast with the dragon lady". Breakfast was some scrambled eggs, turkey bacon and wheat toast. They worked together to clean the small kitchen and Marcia said soon afterwards that she needed to check in at work remotely from her office condo and conduct an afternoon yoga session, but she promised to return and cook him a proper dinner tonight. "Of course it won't be very hard to top popcorn" she laughed. She kissed him lightly on the cheek, hugged him goodbye and was out the door.

Wes was anxious all day. He was struggling with how to break it to Marcia that he needed to be moving on with his plans before one of those infamous Minnesota winter storms set in. He loved the brief time they had spent together but he was a man on a mission and she had a life to resurrect here in Minneapolis. He busied himself with his Rand McNally map again, plotting his course to his next destination. He spent the afternoon gathering his gear from underneath his bed and cleaning his pistol and sniper rifle, making sure that his scopes were clean and his night vision goggles were functioning. The afternoon raced by and when he heard a knock on the door around 4:00 p.m. he gave a start. He had been so engrossed in cleaning his equipment he hadn't heard anyone pull up. His senses were on high alert and he cautiously peeked out his window. Marcia was perched on the steps with a couple of bags. He breathed a sigh of relief and welcomed her in. He had missed her. She made herself at home in the kitchen while Wes showered and by the time he finished shaving she had whipped together a great beet & kale salad, some whole grain pasta with shallots, tomatoes and basil, and a beautiful piece of rare tuna topped the dish. An Oregonian Pinot Noir was served with the meal and at the end Wes pushed his chair back in great appreciation. "No wonder you look so damned good. If you eat like this every day you'll live to be a hundred, and still teaching yoga". She soaked up the praise and smiled coyly. "A little preventative maintenance goes a long way. I make it a point to do something good for myself every single day". After dinner they teamed up on the dishes again and Wes guided Marcia over to the couch. He broke out his snifters and poured them each a couple of fingers of Couvoissier. They toasted their reunion and kicked back to savor the smokey wooden flavors of their drink and allow the meal to settle.

Once again they cuddled on the couch to catch the news and once again the lead story was the nationwide manhunt for the vigilante. Little more had been learned which only helped the mystique of the killer's reputation grow. Some creative journalist had dubbed him "The Specter" in one of his stories and the nickname was beginning to stick. More than thirty victims in various states or injury and almost all with rap sheets and heavy criminal ties. The dregs of society. And yet only the vaguest description could be offered of a man with no ethnicity and no distinguishing characteristics. Op Ed pages on the backs of newspapers across the country began to publish opinion pieces from all manners of citizens about how "The Specter" was doing the work of the police. Efforts by liberal factions to defund police and ban guns from San Francisco to New York had millions of Americans incensed over the past year and now they seemingly had a champion. As news turned to the weather, Marcia got up, retrieved her tote bag headed to the bathroom to get ready for bed. Not a word had been spoken between the two about plans for the night. Nothing it seemed needed to be said. When she finished her preparations she stepped out to give Wes his turn and the effect was stunning. Long flowing hair pulled back into a bow, a pert set of ample breasts pressed against a sheer gown, and long athletic legs tucked under a short nightie was almost more than Wes could stand. She smiled seductively and turned to go into the bedroom. "I'll see you when you are ready", she offered back over her shoulder, and sashayed into the back. Wes didn't need further invitation and wasted no time in getting ready for bed himself and then snuggling in beside Marcia. Their lovemaking was long, passionate and exhilarating. It released an explosion of emotions that both had long suppressed. By the time it was over they collapsed with fatigue and neither twitched a muscle until late the following morning.

CHAPTER 16

CHICAGO METRO P.D.

MARK RAYMOND WAS EXHAUSTED - and frustrated. He had spent days heading the crime task force and coordinating all of the law enforcement and intel agencies that were working the case. As he commanded the head of the War Room and addressed the thirty or so men and women assembled, his frustration was evident. He pivoted to the large White Board behind him and used his pointer, tapping on the screen to emphasize the enlarged photos from the five different crime scenes. "Middleton, Ohio, Florence, Kentucky, Louisville, Kentucky, and now Chicago. Ladies & Gentlemen we have five different crime scenes within a week of each other. Each of you has been on an investigative team at one or more of these sites and yet the most we have so far is the specter of a ghost; just the vaguest description of someone who has access to some pretty high tech shit, who knows how to use it, and knows how to stay off the radar. We have very little to go on, but as of this afternoon our team based here in Chicago has given us our first little sliver of hope. After a tedious search of all the camera footage from the "EL" trains for the past week, they have come up with a morsel of a clue by focusing on any individuals exiting the train station nearest the crime scene. Over four consecutive days they noted a man of medium build, medium height, wearing dark clothes, a dark hat and a mask disembark the train platform at West Garfield Park. Subsequent video footage from a few shops along the route from the station to the crime scene showed this same figure always headed in the general vicinity where the explosion occurred. On his final trip he carried a dark rucksack on his back. He always took the same rail back at the end of the day and additional footage has tracked him on the red line though the downtown loop and back north to the Logan Park Station. We have tried facial recognition software but we can't get a good enough look to find a match. That is precious little to go on but it's all we have for now. I will begin to shift more of our resources to the northwest suburbs, and specifically the Logan Park station to see if we can spot him. In the meantime I want to introduce a new member of our team, Mr. Eric Carlson Chief of Staff with the National Security Agency".

"Good Afternoon" began Mr. Carlson. "As Special Agent Raymond noted I am with NSA and have been called in to assist with this crucial investigation. All of you have a pretty good idea what resources the NSA can bring to bear. But trust me, none of you know the depth of our surveilling talents because it's highly controversial and highly suppressed. We have been called the most secretive agency in the world, and that's not boasting. We fly well below the radar because in order to be effective we have to. With proper government authorization, we can listen in on every conversation, we can download any data, we can look back through your cameras and we can manipulate your computers. At the highest levels this is done through our Supercomputer based in Northeast

Massachusetts. This computer stands fifteen stories tall and is housed in a sub zero temperature concrete vault because of the incredible heat that it generates with all of its computing tasks. Basically it tracks everything. We ask it questions, we analyze the data, and we glean answers. When we are called in to work a case like this we are looking for any lines of chatter. We mined the metro area the day before and the day after the crime here in Chicago but found no evidence of a coordinated communication effort. In addition we sifted through computer data, internet traffic patterns, GPS usage as well as audio and video footage. I can tell you that whoever is behind this is one smart cookie and knows how to avoid leaving any electronic footprint. But we will continue to work this case with you until we put this criminal behind bars. In these times you cannot disappear from the planet. Sooner or later he will slip up. He will need to access cash, he will have to refuel, eat, sleep and any other number of things that leave evidence of his location, his habits, his contacts. He will leave an electronic footprint and once he does we will find him. Thank you for your time and commitment to this and stay focused.

CHAPTER 17

CHILLIN'

ONCE AGAIN WES was the first to stir after a night that left them both totally and incredibly spent. He tried to quietly slip out of the bed but felt a hand grab him. "Don't be silly", she giggled and pulled him back underneath the covers. He rolled over to face her and her gaze was locked onto him with those remarkable emerald eyes that seemed to entirely drink him in. Those eyes got him every time. The sensation of her touch still made his skin tingle and stirred his butterflies to a new dimension. He couldn't believe his good fortune. He had always been one to hop quickly out of a cold and lonely bed each morning and methodically get his day going. Now, nothing pleased him more than to lie back down with Marcia. They didn't do anything more than just lay there and snuggle and talk for hours. No questions, no complications, no commitments; just a lot of whimsical small talk and a little nuzzling for good measure.

After several hours Wes felt it was time to discuss what was to happen next. He pulled away from Marcia, looked directly into her eyes and lowered his voice with a note of seriousness in it. "Marcia", he said, but she cut him short. She recognized the change in him immediately and guessed its intent. She said "don't, let's hold off until after breakfast" she pleaded. How could he refuse? They clasped each other tightly, allowing all of their emotions to release in a fevered lovemaking session until the sheets were soaked with sweat. They showered together and then Wes started breakfast while Marcia busied with the linens. She had the foresight to buy some breakfast goods yesterday and they ate bran muffins with some fruit and stalled conversation a little longer over a fresh pot of coffee. Once breakfast was done and the dishes cleared away they held hands and walked together over to the couch. "This has been amazing for me Marcia", said Wes, " and you have given me several incredible days. Now I need to let you return to your life here in Minneapolis. You have a job, you have a life here, friends, and probably a yoga group that I am sure misses you a whole lot right now. I am on this journey to find myself and for the first time in my entire life I have the freedom to do just that. I need to work some things out in my head. Marcia did not respond, nor did she meet his eyes. She sat silently for a moment with head bowed and hands clasped in her lap. Finally she took a deep breath and looked at him. "My life here has not been the same since Frank was murdered. For that matter, the city is not the same. This summer riots have stained this town and the forced immigration has angered both the native citizens and Somali and Sudanese alike. This is not the town we grew up in Wes. This short time with you has helped to heal a wound and to give me hope, and I am so grateful. As for my job, I work remotely from the office and I can continue to do that. It is all so new right now but I don't want this to end. Is that too forward of me? If it is I apologize". Wes was torn. He did not want it to end either but he sure didn't want to involve Marcia in this reckless life he had currently chosen for himself. She was too good a person and he couldn't be sure how she would accept what he was doing. He argued that he needed a lot of personal time and he wouldn't want to shut her out. She countered that she could occupy herself with her work on her laptop and finish a book that she was writing. She assured him that she wouldn't be a stone around his neck in any way or he could put her on the next plane home. He chuckled at that notion but was smitten and reluctantly agreed, figuring that he would find some way to hide what his real motive was. Marcia spent the rest of the day gathering the clothes that would fit in the bedroom closet, organizing her toiletries, and making arrangements to "button up" the condo for the winter. She was back before dark and they enjoyed a quiet meal together while the widescreen TV provided an update on the nationwide manhunt for "Specter". Wes shook his head as he flipped to other news channels and saw the same news. Marcia didn't share his point of view. "Wes, these people are no different than the thugs that killed Frank. I would take my revenge out on those punks in a heartbeat if given the chance." Wes smiled inwardly and thought that things might just have become a little easier. Maybe we all have a little vigilante in us, thought Wes.

CHAPTER 18

WESTBOUND

"WESTWARD HO" beamed Wes as he sat perched high and proud in his captain's seat commanding his luxury coach west on Interstate 90 out of Minneapolis..... destination, Sioux Falls. It was going to be an easy days' drive of no more than 250 miles. He had identified another "dry" RV park on the outskirts of the town and would easily be there by early afternoon. The 500 h.p. Cummins diesel engine sat on a Spartan chassis which provided a quiet, stable ride. A spectacular floor plan included marble countertops, leather furniture and high gloss porcelain floor tiles. He had his satellite radio signal tuned into Yacht Rock radio "for the people who don't have to work too hard" and Steely Dan was blasting through his Bose surround sound speakers. Marcia was enjoying every moment and was occupied in the back putting her woman's touch on Wes' rolling bachelor's pad. Life was indeed good. After several hours of driving across the western plains of Minnesota Wes spotted a road sign announcing that they were leaving Yellow Medicine County and heading into Chippewa County. The only town on the map in this area was Granite Falls, 12 miles away. That would be a good time to stop, top off the tank and hit the restroom, he thought. He remembered briefly from his college days that it was a picturesque little town of about 3000 people on the Minnesota River that was known for its huge deposits of granite which stood in large outcroppings high above the river. His scout troop had done a one-week camping trip to the area when he was 12 and he remembered learning to canoe along the river. As he slowed upon entering the outskirts of town he spotted a Kwik E Mart that was large enough to easily accommodate his rig. Besides, they advertised fresh deer jerky and it would be an interesting change to his diet. He manoeuvred the RV to the outermost pumps near the highway, parked, and casually looked for cameras. None were evident. He knew that convenient stores were too often handy targets for robberies and therefore equipped with CCTV security. From all appearances, nobody in the quaint, little township of Granite Falls seemed too concerned about that. Nonetheless Wes maintained his low profile as the man in black.

As Marcia stepped from the coach to use the facilities Wes handed her a hundred dollar bill and asked if she would grab a couple of jerkies and a couple of Powerades and put the rest towards diesel on pump #8. She declined the cash, "look Wes, we are in this together and I would like to contribute to some of the expenses". He hesitated but agreed and said "only if you don't use a card, use cash. And I wonder if you would mind putting on a hat and some sunglasses". Marcia was surprised but didn't argue. She had loaded up with cash before leaving Minneapolis. She continued on into the store and was caught a little off guard at the sound of East Indian music playing fairly loudly. It was not uncommon around the Twin Cities to see minorities running registers at convenience stores but this was a long way from the urban sprawl. The attendants' name tag read

Ravi Patel and Mr. Patel had that all too familiar disinterested look of one who is bored out of his mind with his mundane job. He barely looked up as she paid for the drinks and snacks, put them in her satchel and asked him to put the remainder on pump #8. She could not have guessed how fortunate his indifference was for her. She stepped out front, signaled to Wes to fill up and continued on into the restroom. Several minutes later after freshening her make up she exited the store and noticed a man with his back to her confronting Wes as he was screwing the fuel cap back on. The closer she got, she more she realized that something was amiss. Wes was in a defensive mode with his arms halfway in the air and the man had raised a pistol at his head. Wes had slowly reached for his back pocket and prepared to hand the man his wallet. He glanced beyond the robber and noticed Marcia approaching from behind and was surprised to see her draw a gun from her pocketbook. The next moment all happened in a flash. He shook his head to her and mouthed the word "no" as she drew and fired a round from a small caliber weapon directly into the man's back. He went down immediately. The two stood in stunned silence for a few seconds before Wes gained his composure and said "get in the RV now". "Wes it was self defense", she said. "We know that but they don't, there are no witnesses and we don't need to spend the next two days here arguing our case to the local good old boys. Nobody saw this, it looks like the attendant is oblivious, let's go", he said. They scurried into the coach and got on the road without further incident. Wes pushed the speed limit to the max and once again consulted his Rand McNally to find connecting roads south off of the Interstate.

The two rode in silence, both stunned by what had just happened and not able to find words for it. Marcia sat in the passenger seat staring out the large front window, transfixed by what she had just done.Wes continued in a south southwest direction, staying on secondary highways, consulting his map and switching roads at every opportunity. He wanted to put as much distance between them and the Kwik E Mart as he could. He reasoned that he and his rig were not on camera, that the RV had not been parked in line of sight with the store attendant, and that there were no witnesses. The attendant likely would not know what vehicle Marcia was in, would have trouble describing her from their brief encounter, and there was no electronic trace on their purchase. At worst, he thought it would take some time for law enforcement and its likely meager resources this far out to analyze the situation and put on an APB. He hoped that a real life "Barney Fife" type was on duty and would be in way over his head on his unusual event. Sioux Falls was much too close for comfort however so he drove well into the night and finally settled into a truck plaza north of Lincoln, Nebraska where they settled in late that night.

CHAPTER 19

GRANITE FALLS

SINCE ITS INCEPTION IN 1872, the sleepy little township of Granite Falls, Minnesota had never seen anything even remotely on the scale of what was taking place right now. The Kwik E Mart was surrounded by police vehicles, an ambulance, several dark suburban SUVs and of course the local media hoping to get a scoop before the nightly news aired. A camera truck was poised nearby with a cameraman on top filming and sending footage back to his parent TV station. Crime scene tape ringed the entire property and investigators checked off their duty lists. The scene had been photographed and sifted through for evidence. The body had been examined for physical evidence and the cause of death was determined as a single gunshot wound in the back, fired from a small caliber weapon at close range. The body was moved to the ambulance and in its place was a chalk outline. If in fact Granite Falls was a town of 3000, then at least 2900 of them were there, or so it seemed. Law enforcement did its best to keep the curious rabble from overrunning the crime scene tape and contaminating the scene. Detectives were still questioning Mr. Patel who was pathetically short of actionable intelligence. A passerby had alerted him of the body out front, he said. His last customer was a lady, perhaps of middle age. No further description, no camera footage, no credit card purchase, no idea what vehicle she was in, which direction it was headed and if she was alone. Patel said he heard no gunshot but noted that the alleged killer purchased nearly $90 of diesel fuel so she had to be in a large truck or RV.

The body contained no identification but a handgun was found in close proximity and the local police knew the deceased well. He was Jadaveous Cornell, a local petty crook with a long rap-sheet of small time crimes from breaking and entering to small drug dealing. The weapon was stolen during a home break-in that was reported by its owner a couple of weeks prior. The Medical Examiner surmised that Mr. Cornell's death was likely long and painful. The bullet entered mid-spine and continued through his right lung, causing it to deflate. It would have taken him several minutes to suffocate while lying immobile due to spine laceration. Suddenly a cry erupted as Mrs. Odessa Williams had been escorted in to identify her son. She sobbed uncontrollably as she lay across his prone figure on the gurney. Soon the body was taken away for a toxicology exam to see if there was evidence of drugs or alcohol in the deceased. Law enforcement was frustrated at the lack of evidence and when the police chief was asked if he wanted to put out an APB to keep on the lookout, he cynically said "to be on a lookout for what? A truck on the interstate or an RV, driven by whom, headed which direction and how long ago?". Soon the crowd began to disperse, and Granite Falls' fifteen minutes of fame quickly waned.

CHAPTER 20

LINCOLN, NEBRASKA

WES EASED his RV into a parking space in the truck plaza later that evening as far from the building and from cameras as possible. Marcia began preparing a vegetarian chili while Wes set up the rig for the evening. He popped open a bottle of Chardonnay about the time the chili was ready and two of them sat in a relative silence at the table, each waiting for the other to talk about the shooting. The news on the widescreen TV helped ease the silence and, as usual, the poll numbers indicated a continued drop in the Biden administrations' handling of the economy, foreign affairs, immigration, supply chain issues and every other topic which contributed to the lowest approval rating of any modern day President. Local news followed with a story on the Nebraska Cornhuskers promising football season and then transitioned to a weather update with mention of a chance for the season's first snowfall. The next story was breaking news out of Granite Falls and the killing of a young black male. In and of itself, the story would probably not have rated news on a national scale were it not for two very separate reasons. Al Sharpton was being interviewed from his New York office and was decrying the killing as yet another example of racism. A young black male left for dead and no evidence gathered, he was heard yelling over the microphone to a small crowd in front of his posh Manhattan office. The suggestion was that the killer was white and therefore the cover-up of any evidence. This despite the fact that no killer had been identified. Contrary to that, FBI Special Investigator Mark Raymond and some of his team had flown over to the site when news of the killing broke. What intrigued them was the "MO", or method of operation. Another deceased with a rap sheet, killed with a small hand gun, no witness and an incredible lack of clues. It was a little bit of a reach to tie this into their other investigations yet, but the path of victims had continued west and they could leave no stone unturned. Besides, they had turned up nothing else on the Specter.

Marcia was the first to suggest that they turn off the news and discuss what had happened earlier that morning. Wes obliged and they retired to the couch. "I acted without thinking Wes. I often wondered if I could shoot someone after seeing my husband killed but I was never sure that I would be up to it. Then when I saw that man with a gun pointed at your head I acted upon instinct. I lost one good man and I could not imagine losing another. I have been carrying this gun in my purse since Frank's death. Part of me hoped I would never have to use it. Another part of me longed to seek revenge on Frank's killers. She broke down sobbing and Wes held her tightly for a few short minutes while she got it all out. "First of all, thank you. I don't know what would have come of that situation but you may have saved my life", Wes said. "And secondly, you showed guts and you did the right thing. All you did was eliminate one more punk from the streets and we should all be grateful to you. Now I think it's time for me to tell you about what I have been doing and why I asked you to use cash today and wear a ball-cap in that quick mart." Wes proceeded to tell Marcia everything from his years of frustration with law enforcement to his desire to make some amends to people who had been wronged. He detailed each of his stops since leaving Ohio and told how he had began his vengeance.. As he spoke he watched Marcia's eyes register from shock to concern and eventually to what just might be admiration. She sat quietly and let Wes relate his entire story. When he finished, she remained silent for a moment, long enough so that Wes became concerned and wondered if he had spilled the beans too early. Finally he said "do you hate me for what I have done? Do you want me to take you back to Minneapolis?". Marcia formed a easy smile and said "what, and ruin a modern day Bonnie & Clyde story? Not a chance." They finished off the bottle of wine and retired to bed embracing each other closely after a long and emotionally exhausting day.

CHAPTER 21

ON THE ROAD AGAIN

WES INSTINCTIVELY KNEW that the day would eventually come when no matter how careful he was, he could not outsmart the system. All the resources were stacked in their favor. They owned all of the latest technology, so much of which he likely knew nothing about. They held all the cards and so it was just a matter of time before they caught up with him. And so it was that somewhere in the earliest hours of that next morning a dark figure loomed over him and as he sensed it begin to descend upon him he defensively threw up his arms and tried to wrestle his way up out of the bed. But his wrists were quickly pinned back either side of his head and a weight sat on his chest. He struggled violently until he heard a soft "stop". It was a females' voice, a familiar one, and he shook himself from his nightmare and into consciousness to realize that Marcia was straddling him and had him pinned to the mattress; her knees on his wrists, her hands pinning his shoulders. My God that woman is strong, was his very first waking thought, and then he happily surrendered. She lowered herself on him when he ceased fighting and gently caressed his face, softly kissed his forehead, his lips, his neck and then slowly and passionately gave herself to him completely. They lay spent until the first rays of daylight peeked through the sheers. Soon Wes mustered the energy to get up and start a pot of coffee while Marcia was first to the shower. As the coffee brewed Wes flipped on the TV to see if there was further mention of Granite Falls. Instead, news coverage was reporting an MS 13 killing in Lincoln last night. The story gave a background on the international crime gang that was formed in the barrios of L.A. in the 70s by El Salvadoran immigrants. Reportedly, gangs now populated 46 states and worked with the cartels in running drugs, arms, human trafficking and murder for hire. The victims were usually killed with a machete. Last night's crime left two men dead, both apparently beheaded by a machete and both bodies were covered in tattoos typical of MS 13 gang members. Early speculation was that these two had probably tried to leave the gang and it cost them their lives. Wes shuddered and was shaking his head in disgust when Marcia stepped out in her robe and her hair wrapped in a towel on top of her head. He marveled at how cute she was even swathed in towels. "How is our notoriety going? Any mention of us this morning, she quipped?". "No but it looks like there is no shortage of potential candidates", answered Wes.He grabbed the remote and killed the TV while giving her a recap of the story. Marcia listened in horror and shuddered. "Wes I'm scared" she said. "Everyone's scared", he countered. "Everyone's always scared. We have all been scared since you and I were kids. Back then it was the Soviets, the threat of a nuclear bomb, underground fallout shelters, training in junior high school to dive under our desks when the alarm rang; then the anarchy of Vietnam, gas rationing, 9/11." Wes was angry at the state of America and saw a nation edging towards the dark precipice of destruction. He remembered at that moment reading Dante in college and how he had noted that hell was not one place but many. Whether it was MS gang members in Lincoln, the rabble in Chicago, or the cold blooded killers who took Marcia's husband life for a measly forty bucks, crime was out of control. And America could not begin to repair itself without eliminating drugs, gangs, cartels and changing policy in liberally run cities that allowed sanctuary to criminals and illegals. Money that should be spent on science and education and helping the mentally ill was going towards providing free, clean hypodermic needles to the hordes of homeless on the downtown streets. The world had gone mad.

Marcia showed that her skills in the kitchen were equal to those in the bedroom as she whipped up a batter of buckwheat pancakes and rinsed some fresh blueberries while Wes showered. They ate slowly, enjoying every morsel and talked about their next destination. Wes was really getting used to this freedom of the road and Marcia had proven to be a dynamic companion. "I think we keep heading west and see what opportunities lie out there", said Wes. I have never been to California" "Does this mean you aren't throwing me out", laughed Marcia. "After that gymnastics session last night I would be afraid to for fear of you kicking my ass", countered Wes. They both had a good laugh at the expense of each other and cleared away the dishes together.

Marcia's cell phone rang a moment later as Wes was activating the sliders and trimming down the RV for the road. He noted the look of concern as she pressed her ear close and then she put it on speaker phone. "Are you Marcia Brombauer"? "Yes I am", she answered. "Can you verify your home address for us", to which she gave the proper answer. "What is this all about"? she asked. The caller identified himself as Homicide Investigator John Autry of the Minneapolis Police Department and said he and his team had been working a recent murder case in the city and yesterday they apprehended two suspects. He noted that the ballistics from the round matched those found in her husband's body. "Are you sure" gasped Marcia. "Yes, in fact the two agreed to confess to killing your husband for a plea deal", said Autry. "Tell me what that means" she asked. He answered that if they gave a confession and, depending on what the judge and the lawyers construct, with much haggling yet to be done, they could be locked up for about 12 years and then, pending good behavior, could be released. Marcia was shocked but hid her anger. "I would like to have some say-so in this and meet his killers. What can I do"? "There is an arraignment next Tuesday at 2:00 p.m. in the Minneapolis District Court. You are welcome to be there" finished Autry. "And I will be there", said Marcia and hung up. She sat a moment, gathering herself, then turned to Wes and said "I have to go and I don't want to interfere with your plans so can you put me on an airplane?" "Nonsense", "I'm going back with you", he said. She jumped up and hugged him and he willingly let her fawn all over him for a moment, thinking that this may work well in his plans and perhaps also throw his pursuers a little curve.

CHAPTER 22

SPECTER

WES AND MARCIA readied the coach and slowly retraced their route back towards Minneapolis. Wes drove along Interstate 80 East just under the speed limit as Marcia tidied up and had the TV tuned to Fox News to occupy her thoughts and receive any further word on the investigation of "the Specter". Around mid-morning an update on the story of the investigation was aired. Nobody likes to admit defeat, least of all politicians and law enforcement and government officials. Therefore it was a very tepid update on the killings across Kentucky, Chicago and potentially Granite Falls. Special Investigator Raymond did not outwardly express his lack of progress during this exclusive interview but his tone was all telling. He once again asked for community support if anyone had information, but he had so little to offer in terms of evidence that appeared this was a futile exercise thus far. The FBI, the intelligence agencies and local law enforcement were all present for the press conference. Questions were directed to each from the assembly of reporters but there was no takeaway from this other than that they feared this vigilante was not done. The first signs of outward support for the mysterious assassin ringed the crowd. Hand held placards touted "let's go Specter". Scattered chants were heard across the assembly, "Specter, Specter, Specter". This added to the frustration of law enforcement and when Raymond once again had the podium he had to denounce anyone taking the law into his own hands. He understood public sentiment as crime rose, police departments were defunded, an overreaching government was trying to ban gun sales and citizens felt vulnerable for the first time in their lives. Raymond mouthed the usual promises......"we condemn these crimes in the strongest terms", "we will bring these criminals to justice", and of course "our prayers go out to the families", but inwardly he knew that they were getting no closer.

When Marcia finally shut off the TV and climbed up front into the passenger seat Wes could not help but notice how quiet she was and suspected that she was thinking about the phone call earlier that morning. He let her reflect for a while and then, not knowing what else to do, he reached over and put a hand on her arm and asked "do you want to talk about it?" She looked at him and forced a smile then looked straight ahead. "Frank wasn't yet fifty. So strong and vital and had everything to live for. He kissed me on his way out the door that morning and it was the last time I ever saw him alive", she said, staring out the windshield into the horrors of her past. Wes murmured "I'm so very sorry Marcia". "The most unbelievable thing is that when something so unimaginable happens, a thing that kills you inside, you keep breathing and your heart beats and you still live. Time goes on", she said. Wes had to fight his own feelings, and they were many. He wanted to comfort her. He wanted to take revenge out on someone. "It's been a long time since I thought about this, but that phone call stirred up all my emotions again", said Marcia. She described all of her fantasies of killing the two men who killed her husband. "What can I do" responded Wes. "Will you come into the courtroom with me?", she answered. "I cannot do that and I think you know why. But I will be waiting on the courthouse steps for you when you come out." She smiled and they lapsed into silence. Marcia's pain had permeated the RV and Wes could see the violent imagery she had drawn up of her husband's execution. Those images followed him along the interstate for some time as he formulated his next move.

CHAPTER 23

MINNEAPOLIS

THE HENNIPEN COUNTY COURTHOUSE in downtown Minneapolis traced its history back to 1888 when a team of foresighted architects laid out a strategic plan that would eventually encompass the district courts, a public safety sector, a juvenile detention center, an adult detention center, City Hall, the Sheriff's Department and 12 floors of parking spaces. The complex had grown as the city grew and now stretched across more than two square city blocks. Because of the ferocity of Minnesota winters, there was a network of enclosed walkways and tunnels that linked the buildings together. The connecting corridor between the adult detention center and the courthouse was the lone exception to this, an open air breezeway with a small rock courtyard on either side. Prisoners were escorted along this breezeway to the courtrooms by armed Sheriff's deputies. They wore shackles and had hands cuffed behind for safety protocol. On this singular, cold morning a deputy led the two criminals from the jail along the breezeway and to the courtroom, with another deputy trailing. From his position on the sixth floor of the parking deck, Wes knelt between two vehicles with his sniper rifle trained on his targets. His suppressor was attached and he peered through his scope as the men reached the center of the breezeway. With two quick taps for each of the murderers, his task was done in seconds. He broke down his rifle, put the pieces in a backpack and slipped down a back stairwell to the third floor where Marcia's car was parked near the stairwell. He opened the trunk, removed the panel where the spare tire should have been, and in its place he put the backpack. He closed and locked the car and continued down the stairwell to the ground floor and out a back door to 11th Ave. He casually but purposefully wandered due west from the courthouse and was already two blocks away before law enforcement could respond and lock down the building. As he walked, he removed a small sealed packet of hand sanitizer from his jacket pocket and applied it liberally. He threw the empty packet in a trash bin and continued on to Gold Medal Park at 2nd St. and 11th Avenue about 10 blocks from the courthouse where he settled on a bench and began reading his paperback edition of Tom Clancy's latest novel.

Back inside the courthouse Marcia had cleared the security station and was escorted inside the courtroom where she was introduced to the Prosecuting Attorney. He eyed her appreciatively and asked what her interest was in being here. She said that she wanted the opportunity to make her case for a stronger conviction of these hoodlums and to let the court know what she had been through since the killing. He promised to have her heard and as they settled in the front of the courtroom, alarms went off all across the complex. The building was quickly placed in lockdown and nobody was allowed to enter or leave. Each building was secured, all occupants were kept in place, and the parking garage was sealed down. Dogs were brought in and SWAT teams worked every room, every closet in every building as well as the garage levels. CCTV camera footage was gathered and reviewed. Soon word began to spread that the two men who were to be sentenced today had been executed. Facts were scarce but uniformed police officers entered the courtroom and asked Marcia if she had come alone. She said she had. They made her aware of the murders and asked if she knew of anyone who would want them dead. "Other than me" she said, "I'm not aware of anyone else they have wronged but I suspect I'm not the only one. Didn't they both have pretty lengthy rap sheets?". That was confirmed by the officers and they continued to question her and the few others in the room. After more than two hours of questioning, all building occupants were escorted to their cars. A cursory check of the cars was conducted as each was put in their seat and told to exit the parking lot. It was nearly 5:30 p.m. before Marcia pulled out on to 2nd St. and made her way 10 blocks west to the entrance of Gold Medal Park, watching closely behind her in her rearview mirror. She drove slowly, entering into the downtown seven acre park and backed into a corner spot. Darkness was slowly descending as she took her cell phone out of her pocket and called her mother to see how she was managing her troublesome arthritis. Mom was in a retirement home in Mankato and Marcia called weekly to check in. All the time she watched closely to see if there was any unusual activity taking place in front of her, any suspicious cars or pedestrians who hadn't moved in the time that she spoke with her mother. After ten minutes she hung up, turned on her headlights and started the car. Seconds later the passenger door quickly opened and closed just as quickly. Wes slipped into the passenger seat and they returned to Marcia's condo for the night.

CHAPTER 24

DOWNTOWN MINNEAPOLIS

WHEN A HOMICIDE OCCURS on state property, state and local police have the option to invite the FBI in to investigate the murder if they think it is warranted. In this case, FBI Special Investigator Mark Raymond took the lead after being alerted of the killings in Minneapolis and contacted Police Chief Warren "Wiggo" Anderson personally and asked for permission to lead the investigation, as it had all the earmarks of his serial killer. Wiggo was happy to step back and let the big boys bring in their full complement of resources. This execution was a blemish on his jurisdiction and he wanted to clear it up ASAP. Thus far state and local authorities had come up with very little. Both deceased were executed by a sniper and the angle of entry suggested that the shot came from an upper floor of the parking deck about 200' away. It would have taken a trained marksman to pull off a precision killing like this within seconds and leave no trace. Ballistics tests indicated the rounds could have been fired from the same weapon that was used in Chicago to ignite the Sarin gas bomb. Every floor of the parking deck was dusted, sifted through and fingerprinted. There were no empty shell casings, no powder burns along any of the half walls on the open sides of the deck facing the breezeway, and no camera footage of a shooter.

FBI Lead Investigator Mark Raymond was not having a good day. Everyone in the briefing room looked as blank as Agent Raymond felt. He nursed his last sip of lukewarm coffee from his styrofoam cup and sat spinning his black Mont Blanc fountain pen on his red folder as he assembled his thoughts. He and his team had gone over every bit of video footage on the morning of the murder. Nothing caught their attention in the routine pedestrian traffic inside the buildings that morning. The thing that did catch their attention from the parking deck was an image of an average sized man in dark clothing, dark hat, sunglasses and a mask with a backpack on walking along the sixth floor parking deck before he disappeared from camera view. This same figure was later seen on the third floor of the parking deck headed to an exit. He was never filmed entering any of the buildings, which seemed odd, but he could have been headed somewhere besides the county complex. Raymond noted that it looked eerily like the footage they had from the "EL" train in Chicago. But in both cases those images were so indistinct that he could not be certain. He had the best photo of his face that they could obtain but it was abysmal. Not only was he masked, but he also held a phone to his ear, further hiding his face. Raymond had checked in with his tech in Massachusetts and had the SuperComputer run cell traffic for that time and that area but got no chatter of consequence. He surmised that in fact the phone was not used but merely a shield. The suspect also seemed to know the location of all parking deck cameras and how to avoid any good footage. Raymond opened FACE, the agency's facial recognition software and imported the image. The program was amazing and could identify a partial image with 85% accuracy if a mugshot was in the federal database. In this case he struck out. He called his pal Jericho Miles, the FBI's top forensic tech in Quantico, gave him the rap and forwarded the photo. "Give me ten minutes and I'll call you back", said Jericho. Raymond leaned back in his chair, clasped his hands behind his head, put his legs on his desk and stared at the acoustical tile ceiling while he waited. Eight minutes later Jericho called and said "we have zippo Buddy".

Raymond finally stood and addressed his team in the hastily assembled conference room. Updated photos filled the whiteboard. A chalkboard linked all of their previous investigation sites to Minneapolis looking for a pattern. Satellite phones, laps tops and cells and styrofoam coffee cups littered the room. Reporters were wedged at the door looking for a scoop. Investigator Raymond was livid with frustration but managed to show only outward calm. He stood at the front of the room and said "We've got to get a grip on this case, a clue, a witness, a theory or even a confidential source. Anything that holds water. I don't like asking for public help; a posting brings out the kooks and is 99% nonsense, but we are looking for that 1%. Check out your sources, call in favors, no one goes anywhere until we have something with legs." With that the room was immediately abuzz once again and Raymond stalked out.

CHAPTER 25

STREET LIFE

KIM HOLCOMB WAS HOT. Not just a cute type of hot but smokin' drop dead gorgeous hot with a full head of loose ash blonde curls falling around her shoulders, penetrating emerald green eyes and a brilliant white smile full of perfect teeth. The whole effect could stop most men dead in their tracks. Add to that a freakin' killer body for which she had a knack for perfectly accenting with spiked heels, tight jeans and a snug bodice today complimenting every tantalizing curve. Top all of that off with a saucy attitude to match, and most men were intimidated. So Kim had very few dating opportunities and therefore threw herself into her work as a good reporter for the Minneapolis Star Tribune. She had been on that beat for nearly ten years since graduating from the University of Minnesota with a degree in journalism. Now in her early 30s, it was time for her to make a move up the corporate ladder and she was looking for the first good opportunity; the first big story that would be picked up nationally and catapult her career forward with a nationally known by-line.

Kim sat at her desk early that morning thumbing her cell phone when her land line rang. She answered by identifying herself. "I may have something for you" the voice on the other end said. She recognized it as Bruno Tillis, a confidential informant that she had used on occasion to get leads on stories from the streets. The city streets had a life of their own and a few street life folks knew how to work that to their advantage. Bruno was one of them. Kim had developed this shady relationship when she was still in college and hitting the late night bars around town and often scoring a little weed from Bruno and his sort. She left that life far behind but was savvy enough and streetwise enough to know that people like Bruno could prove handy with information from the underworld. Bruno managed a car wash on 11th St. about 2 blocks down from the Hennipen County Courthouse. "Do you want to come to my office and talk about it?" asked Kim. "You know I can't do that, I'm on probation and need to stay low", he said. "What if we meet at Cheddars and you can buy me lunch?" "Couldn't you pick a restaurant with two dollar signs instead of three? I'm on a reporter's salary you know", Kim said, half in jest. "Do you want the information or not"? Was the response. "Sure, what time?". Bruno asked her to be there by two and get a booth as far back in the rear as she could. He added that he would be there shortly after and hung up.

Kim arrived shortly before two and was escorted past a row of bar stools, almost all occupied by guys following sports on the wide screens, to the last booth in the restaurant. "This is perfect", she said, "I'm expecting a gentleman to join me shortly". "Okay Hon", was the reply, "four stars on our great crab cake sandwich today and soup of the day is split pea. Can I get you a drink while you wait?" "Just water for me" she said and glanced around at the dark paneling, the framed photos of sports stars on the wall and the banks of TVs that currently had most customers focusing on the horse races at Saratoga Springs. The bar was nice and had a clubby feel to it. She suspected it was not a regular hangout for Bruno. Minutes later he slid into the booth almost ghostlike and caught her by surprise. The waitress returned with Kim's water and Bruno ordered a Sam Adams Ale draft. The two studied the menu and caught up on small talk, with neither showing much of their poker hand. Once they ordered, Bruno broke the ice and said he saw the appeal for public help on the recent shooting and that he might have something. "What have you got?", asked Kim. "What's it gonna get me?", he responded. "It depends upon how helpful your information is. If anything comes of it, I'll get you some help on your upcoming DUI conviction", said Kim. "Okay" was his response and then proceeded to tell her that he was sitting outside of his car wash the other morning smoking a cigarette when he heard all of the alarms at the courthouse go off. That was pretty unusual, he said, so he was watching in that direction when a man in dark clothing, with his head down and hands in his pockets was walking away from there a little quicker than most people tended walk in the city. He has a nose for the streets and knew when something seemed out of order. He added that the man walked by him on the other side of the street without looking or slowing down. Bruno said he didn't want to get caught up in the middle of something so he waited until he was just past him and snapped his photo with his phone which provided a fairly decent profile. He pulled out his Samsung and showed the image on the cracked and smudged screen. Kim studied it and asked him to send it to her phone. They ate lunch, mostly in silence, and Kim called for the check, saying she had to get back to work. "Is that photo worth a piece of their homemade apple pie?" Bruno pleaded. "Killin' me Bruno, but okay and thanks for the tip. I'll be in touch". She preferred to spend as little time with Bruno as posible and he likely felt the same way about being seen with a reporter. "Okay" he called after her as she exited the booth "but we never had this meeting". "Yep, same as always", she threw over her shoulder and sashayed past the barstools and past several sets of approving eyes.

CHAPTER 26

THE DEAL

KIM RETURNED BACK to her desk among the insanity that made up the newsroom of the Minneapolis Star Tribune. It was a jungle of phones and desks cluttered with lap tops and papers, journalists, reporters, photographers and graphic artists as well as the editing staff. Presiding over this giant floor of insanity was the Editor who had been hammering his people for days to find a scoop on the murder story and, better yet, a link to the Specter. The whole vigilante theory had gone viral and every glimpse of film footage from reporters on the streets now had the mob mentality types in the background cheering for their new hero. America desperately needed a diversion, a reprieve from the political warfare and the grim news that followed the Biden administration each day. An ominous figure looming in the shadows who was exacting revenge and evading the law at every turn was just the delicious morsel of retribution the average Joe in the street hungered for.

Kim had been around the block a time or two before and was a savvy and street smart reporter. She knew how to turn this new piece of information to her advantage and perhaps get the exclusive the Editor was clamoring for. She dialed the number for the FBI hot line and said she had some information on the killing. Her call went though the vetting that every other potential crank call had to run the gauntlet for, until finally her identity and position were verified and she was patched in to Mark Raymond's cell. "Ms. Holcomb, thank you for calling", Raymond said. "I apologize for your wait and I'm sure you must understand that we get flooded with bogus calls when something like this goes out. Do you have something useful for this case?". Kim relayed the story of one of her confidential informants capturing a photo of mysterious man walking away from the county courthouse as the alarms activated. Mr. Raymond was intrigued and asked if she was able to send that photo to him. She told him that she could but in exchange she would like an exclusive on the story if the photo helped and once more information was developed for release. Raymond agreed on the condition that he would proof her story before it was published. She in turn agreed, got his email address and forwarded the photo.

CHAPTER 27

WAUKESHA, WISCONSIN

FBI SPECIAL INVESTIGATOR Mark Raymond received the photo of the suspect from Kim, enlarged it on his screen and cleaned up the image. It was taken from across the street and not a perfect profile, but it was much better than anything he previously had. He entered the photo into the FBI's facial recognition software database and determined that it had no match for any prior criminals. However the software did determine that this was almost certainly a match for the suspect on the "EL" train from Chicago whose image had been captured. Now he had a link to the killings. He called Kim Holcomb and thanked her for the photo and told her to start to develop the story on Specter so he could proof it for content. Kim was ecstatic and marched in to her Editor's office with a photo and a scoop on the story of the Specter, as approved so far by the FBI. He was thrilled to hear about a breakthrough and told her to get busy writing the story and bring it to him before sending it to the FBI. This was the break she was looking for and she buried herself in the details for the rest of the day.

Wes and Marcia knew that it was time to leave Minneapolis. As they sat over coffee in Marcia's condo, watching TV, the news cycle had shifted from the exploits of the Specter to an update on the story of the wacko who drove his red SUV into a crowd during the annual Waukesha, Wisconsin Christmas parade in November. 39 year old Darrell Brooks had killed 6 people and injured 62. He had a long criminal record and was currently being held in the Waukesha jail for trial while his lawyers, and his mother, pleaded for leniency due to mental health issues. Wes and Marcia agreed that this was their next target and prepared to leave for Wisconsin. The RV had become a liability after the incident in Granite Falls in which is was established that the killer purchased 90 dollars of diesel fuel. They stored it in a remote storage lot in St. Paul and hopped in Marcia's Buick Regal heading east to Waukesha, just on the outskirts of Milwaukee. Marcia drove as Wes researched the internet on a burner phone and formulated a plan for Mr. Brooks.

Darrell Brooks was being held in the Waukesha City Jail along with 36 other inmates who were awaiting trial hearings. As with most jails, theirs was located on the bottom floor of the city's municipal county courthouse complex, away from people and with no natural light to brighten its dreary confines. When something as unpleasant as a sewage back-up occurs in a building, it is enough of a distraction to quickly alter all normal activities.

Such was the occasion that following morning when raw sewage flowed from a blockage on the external sewer line in the rear of the city hall back into the jail cells which, of course, being on the lowest level, were the first to note the evidence. The odor and the presence of the sewage spilling across the floors was horrific and prisoners started banging on bars to be rescued. The entire lower floor of criminals was quickly evacuated and moved to a holding cell on the third floor. The corrections office called in its normal contract cleaning crew which performed weekly janitorial services for the building. It also requested extra casual labor staff to squeegee out the accumulated splooge, mop up the residue, and disinfect the entire lower floor. This was without question a serious health issue. Two vans staffed with crews in hazmat suits brought more than a dozen people onto the site and they began to vigorously mop and sanitize the entire lower complex. Nobody could be faulted for not noticing one extra body, dressed like the others, among the work crew who methodically went from cell to cell cleaning while casually taking the opportunity to check the office manifest list of criminals against the cell assignments. He was of medium build and height with no further distinguishing features. No one could have suspected that during his duties he identified the cell of killer Darrell Brooks and while mopping out his cell he discreetly placed an compact explosive under the bed frame. In fact, this same nondescript figure had been monitoring the building all day and found it a simple matter earlier that morning to take a large pipe wrench and rotate the sewage outflow pipe at the back of the building 180 degrees to shut off the valve.

CHAPTER 28

FORK IN THE ROAD

WES AND MARCIA had booked a room at the Fairfield Inn on 6th Avenue for few days. It was conveniently located on the perimeter of the Waukesha city limits, which itself was located conveniently to Milwaukee. The town was quaint and navigable so it was easy to walk around a get a sense of its history. Known for its crystal clear spring water it was often referred to as "spa town" and its make-up was essentially 80% white and 20% black, but civil unrest had never been much of a problem here. The Native Waukesha Indian population had long since left or been relocated to reservations. Waukesha was essentially a working class town of good, honest people with traditional upper midwest values which is why the horror of the murderous assault during its Christmas parade had shocked the town so dramatically.

The day was spectacularly pleasant for late Fall and Wes and Marcia took the opportunity to stroll about the town much like any other middle-aged couple, hand in hand out for a sight-seeing trip. Their route was strategically planned however and included a walk by "The Fork in the Road" restaurant where they had a reservation that night. Marcia had googled its menu and was intrigued by its veal meatloaf and its signature champagne martini. Downtown was diverse, vibrant and bustling with activity. A second google search had indicated it was gentrified now but five years ago it was dangerous after sunset. They passed the restaurant, noting its close proximity to the county courthouse complex where, today, the prisoners would be returned to their regular cells. The process, which Wes knew too well, would be slow and thorough to make sure each prisoner was clean on the transfer. By 9:00 p.m. sharp tonight, all prisoners would be in their cells, doors would be locked, lights would be extinguished and things would once again return to normal. Or so they thought.

After a vigorous day of walking, which both agreed they desperately needed, Wes and Marcia showered, dressed and were looking forward to a good meal tonight. The 7:00 o'clock news was on as they readied to go and the lead story was that yet another casualty from the Christmas parade. This was about a woman who had been in a coma and finally succumbed to her injuries. Wes just stared after the news and shook his head until he heard Marcia say, "that just makes tonight's job easier". The couple strolled through the pleasant night down to "The Fork in the Road" and instantly liked the ambience of the room as they entered. They enjoyed a champagne martini at the bar before dinner and then marveled at the delicious veal meatloaf dish and potatoes au gratin. After dinner they eschewed any desserts, this despite the waiter's best attempt to lure them to the Caramel Creme Brulee'. They were woefully behind on their fitness regimen and needed to claw their way back into shape. It was just after 9:00 p.m. when they exited and began the walk back to the hotel. The walk took them by the courthouse complex and Wes artfully steered them in the shadows between the street lamps without causing attention. As they passed the west side of the complex where the prisoners were kept, he removed a remote activator from his coat pocket. Its maximum effective range was about 200 yards and Wes estimated he was about half that distance from the westernmost wall of the building. He pressed the button, a muffled explosion was heard and they continued their way back to the Fairfield for the night.

CHAPTER 29

THE SCOOP

KIM WORKED LATE into the night pulling together all of the background information that she could get her hands on regarding the two perps who were executed in downtown Minneapolis and cross referencing it with information on the series of other killings that the FBI was chasing. She had managed to wrangle Agent Raymond's personal cell phone number from him and called him that evening asking for any further update for her story. He didn't add much but did tell her he was releasing the photo which she had provided him with to the media in the morning. He sent her electronic confirmation that she could run with her story and the photo in the Star Tribune morning edition. He said she had exclusive rights to the story until tomorrow's media release. She was ecstatic and immediately called her Editor at home and got him to call in and stop the presses so that they could change the lead story for tomorrow morning. Theirs would be the first paper in the country with this latest update on the Specter.

The story splashed front page the next morning in 1.5" inch bold type with Kim's byline just under the headline and below it a somewhat grainy black & white profile photo of the alleged Specter skulking down a downtown Minneapolis city street. Kim had been fidgety with excitement that night and sleep came in short, sporadic naps until she finally gave it up by 4:00 a.m. and put on a pot of coffee. She went to her PC to pull up the morning's E version of the newspaper and read with great appreciation how little editing was done to her story. She fixed herself a good cup of medium roast coffee, plopped her feet up on the desk, and read everything a second time while savoring the steaming cup. This, she thought was just the beginning. This vigilante angle was going to be a major story until he was either caught or disappeared, and she was going to be all over it. Almost on cue, her cell phone buzzed. She looked at the caller I.D., smiled, and answered "good morning agent Raymond, don't you ever sleep"? "Not when there is a killer on the loose", he said, "and it looks like he struck again last night in Wisconsin". She couldn't believe her ears. Special FBI Investigator Mark Raymond was sketchy on the details, as nothing had been released to the public yet, but he did confirm that it looked like another convict was blown up. He said his team was on its way to Waukesha now and he closed by saying "now we are even on favors and good luck with your story". The phone clicked and Kim swallowed down the rest of her coffee while heading to her bedroom to pack a bag.

CHAPTER 30

AMERICA'S DAIRYLAND

IT WAS NEARLY a straight shot southeast of about 320 miles along I-95 from Minneapolis to Waukesha. Agent Raymond and his caravan of dark SUVs posed an ominous spectacle as they traversed across the eastern part of Wisconsin later that morning through the lowlands and the gentle hills that made up the state's landscape. They were running their bubble gum lights on top, but with no sirens at about 80 mph. It was a pretty drive, thought Raymond, and was widely acknowledged as some of world's best farmland. But of course Wisconsin was primarily known as America's dairyland and acclaimed for its cheeses. Wisconsinites were, to a large degree, of hearty German and Eastern European stock. They liked their food and were said to consume 21 million gallons of ice cream annually. They also proudly laid claim to inventing the ice cream sundae. None of that however was worth a spit to Special FBI Investigator Raymond. He just wanted to get his team into town as quickly as possible and comb the bomb site before it got corrupted by unwitting cops.

As luck would have it, the team hit a roadblock of protesters downtown at Badger and 7th and had to navigate around it. "What in the hell?" he half muttered under his breath. He had assumed the town would be in an uproar about the killing, but what were they protesting? This Darrell Brooks guy couldn't have a single sympathetic soul in town after wiping out more than forty of its residents. As they skirted the mob he began to see signs explaining the reason. "Specter for Attorney General" read one. Another read "Defund the police, defend Specter". Many more of its kind were being waved by those in the rally which thankfully was peaceful. My God, he thought, they are getting ahead of us and making a connection to last night's killing and this serial killer who had become bigger than life. The FBI team had been expected and was ushered in to the lower floor where the cells were. The site had been preserved, as requested, and only the body of Mr. Brooks had been carefully photographed and removed so that forensics could begin. That is, what was left of it. DNA testing would confirm the identity and cause of death was not very much was in question.

Wes and Marcia woke early that morning but did not linger over coffee nor did they go down to the hotel's breakfast bar. The less evidence of their presence there, the better, reasoned Wes. He steered the Buick Regal east out of town just as the sun was just beginning to peek over the horizon. They were headed right into it and he had to pull down the visor and don his sunglasses to get through the unfamiliar roads. It had been nearly 10 hours since the bomb detonated and the couple noted a horde of gawkers gathering around the courthouse, likely after hearing the local morning news. "Look", said

Marcia, and pointed to several people carrying signs, one which clearly read "Specter for Man of the Year". "Your popularity grows, do you want to stop and sign a few placards for your adoring throng?" Wes laughed, but nudged the gas pedal just a skooch more and continued out of town without looking back.

CHAPTER 31

ANYTHING BUT LIVER

KIM WAS on the road to Waukesha by 6:00 a.m. She expected to arrive around noon so she made a courtesy call to the editor of the Milwaukee Journal Sentinel to make him aware that she would be in town to follow up on her story about the Minneapolis killings and its potential link to the Waukesha bombing last night. Sam Proctor was fairly young to be a newspaper editor but he had been groomed for the position after getting his degree in Journalism at the University of Wisconsin - Madison, and then a decade in the trenches with the Journal Sentinel as a journalist. He looked poised for a promising career in the newspaper industry, as corporate ownership felt that he had his finger on the pulse of the many changes that needed to take place in that business for it to survive. He took Kim's call and was grateful for her professional courtesy. He had read her blockbuster account of the Specter on the newswire earlier that morning. It was well written and loaded with intrigue, and the photo of the shadowy figure really whet the reader's appetite for a good mystery. He invited her to drop into his office to say hello when she arrived and he would make a desk available for her while she was in town.

Kim had "dressed down" for the road trip, but even in flat, white, canvas shoes, jeans and a University of Minnesota sweatshirt on she was a looker. More than a few curious sets of eyes looked her over as she was directed to Sam's office. Sam was a striking gentleman himself and presented a good first impression to his visitor. His strong handshake told Kim that he was probably a golfer, but most certainly athletic, and his presence did nothing to belie that. His jet blue eyes met hers unflinchingly and they never wavered. With his easy demeanor, Kim decided instantly that she liked him. She handed him her card and he offered her a chair at his desk and quickly went over protocol for visiting reporters. When their conversation finished he showed Kim to her desk, situated among the myriad of others that characteristically made up a newsroom. Before he left, he asked her if she would give him an update on any progress she made by the end of the day. Kim said it was now past lunch time and she would likely have no time to eat until dinner later that night. "Maybe we could meet and update each other over dinner. I'll be starving and I'll bet you probably know all the best places", she said. Sam was flattered but was ready. "It may improve my reputation to have a dinner date with the prettiest girl in Wisconsin. What kind of food do you like?" "Anything but liver" was her answer and Sam said he had just the place. Kim told him she was staying at the Fairfield and could probably be ready by 7:00. "I'll be the one with the famished look on my face in case you've forgotten how I look". It was a loaded comment and again Sam was ready "fat chance" he smiled, "I'll pick you up out front".

Sam pulled up to the hotel porta cochere promptly at 7:00

and Kim stepped out looking like she could step right onto the cover of Vogue. "You look sensational", he admired. She smiled warmly and accepted the compliment while silently approving how he looked like he had just come from a shopping spree at Saville Row in London. She had been working too hard and had been neglecting her social life for far too long. This night had all the earmarks of a delightful night out. They made small "feeling out" talk on the way over to "Angelinas"; a favorite of Sam's because of its great wine list and upscale Italian food. Once at the restaurant they were escorted to a cozy little table for two in a corner nook. Sam had called ahead earlier that day to ask his friend and owner Mario Puzo to make sure they got special service. Menus were presented and Sam and Kim ordered martinis; his Tanqueray Gin, hers Absolut Vodka, both straight up and dirty. Kim never opened her menu. "Would you order for us, I like anything Italian and you have the advantage of knowing this place", offered Kim. "Of course, they have a great liver dish here", joked Sam. That earned him a soft punch on the arm. They had Caesar Salad prepared flawlessly table-side by their waiter, Duncan, followed by a delightful shrimp pasta dish with sun-dried tomatoes and seasoned just right with basil, garlic and lemon. Sam ordered a bottle of his favorite wine, a Benovia Chenin Blanc from the Russian River Valley. Once dinner was finished and the waiter poured the last of the wine into their glasses, the two were left to discuss what they had learned in the course of the day. The warm "glow" from the martinis and the wine set the stage for a wonderful evening of conversation.

CHAPTER 32

BONNIE & CLYDE

WHILE THE FBI investigative team sifted through the debris from the jail bombing, Mark Raymond and his Deputy Director methodically went through the spools of CCTV video footage from the time the sewage back-up occurred until after the bomb exploded. It was pretty well established by the FBI that the sewer problem was not coincidence, but well planned and used as a method to plant an explosive. Who and how was still in question and both investigators slowly rolled the video forward trying to pinpoint a suspect. With more than a dozen men in hazmat suits it was proving an impossible task to identify anyone. The contract cleaning service had paid seven of its own crew to clean and hired an additional seven from its casual labor force. And yet Mark and his Deputy Director, Phillip Gaddy, had confirmed there were fifteen different workmen on video cleaning that day. Camera footage was not intrusive enough to establish which had planted a bomb. Mark continued to review more video coverage from inside the jail and had Director Gaddy go through the video from the courthouse street cameras to see if he could pick up anything.

"Boss, you may want to come and look at this", Gaddy said later that afternoon. He cued up a thirty second video of the street in front of the courthouse from just moments before the explosion until the moment that it occurred. Just before detonation, an indistinct figure of medium height and medium build, in a knee length heavy coat and fedora was filmed passing by. He was not alone. On his elbow was a woman also in a heavy coat and partially obscuring the man from the camera. They nonchalantly kept to the shadows between the street lamps and headed east on 11th after detonation. Most curious was the fact that the camera picked up the explosion and yet the couple never halted their steps or looked back. Mark Raymond enlarged the image and sent it to Quantico to run through FACE, the facial recognition program again to see if they could get a match with the previous photos. After ten minutes FBI headquarters called back to say it was not able to either dismiss or confirm that this was the same man. "Damn" fumed Raymond, "this guy is good. Let's canvas all of the hotels in walking distance in the direction they were heading and get their guest lists. Let's see if we can come up with something. I know in my gut this is our guy and now we have him with a woman again after that shooting in Granite Falls. Looks like we have a real modern day Bonnie & Clyde on our hands".

Grainy black & white images of the Specter began to appear everywhere, and the fact that each one was of a ghost-like figure with no distinctive traits just made the story more appealing. This was a splendid gift to the media and the tabloids. The morning and evening news cycles had a field day. Law enforcement from the Justice Department on down to the local precincts tried their best to condemn him, but it only had the opposite effect. Theories abounded. Surely with his knowledge of weapons, explosives, surveillance equipment and the ability to remain elusive pointed to the fact that he was former Special Forces guy. Maybe a Green Beret, or a member of Seal Team 6, or at the very least, a specially trained government agent gone rogue like Jason Bourne. What a delicious story and people couldn't get enough of it. Every suspected killing of his was linked to the next one and it was well documented that each victim had criminal ties. Law abiding citizens loved it and praised him. He was becoming a national hero and even iconic on the world stage. The latest juicy scoop on the story hit sensationally the next morning on the front page of both the Minneapolis Star Tribune and the Milwaukee Journal Sentinel in a collaborative effort by the two. The large headlines read **"Bonnie & Clyde resurrected?",** and the byline was that of Kim Holcomb, the young journalist who first produced an alleged image of Specter, mentioned a potential female accomplice, and the potential link between the Minneapolis killings and the string of others over the last several weeks.

CHAPTER 33

MOVING DAY

LEAD FBI SPECIAL Investigator Mark Raymond was watching how the media was dealing with the bombing and its potential link to the series of killings and, ultimately, Specter. The headline stories on all news channels and mainstream cable were currently focused on this latest hit. As the reporter on the street in Waukesha stared into the camera and tried to describe the horror, men in dark FBI jackets were bagging and tagging evidence, all of this was accompanied by the crackle and squelch of squad car radios in the background. Mark just shook his head and turned it off. He knew the time was nearing for his team to go back to D.C. They had nothing further to go on. They had grilled fellow jail mates of Brooks', the employees of the detention center, and all fourteen men on the sewage cleaning crew and again came up empty. Specter had once again seemingly given a big middle finger to the agency. Mark called for a wrap-up meeting at the courthouse late that morning in Conference Room A. It seemed like an army of men and women from every walk of law enforcement was assembled in the room. "Ladies & gentlemen, tomorrow we clear this site and my team will relocate back to Washington. But know that this case has taken on the highest priority at the FBI. Our agency has 35,000 people on the government payroll and, granted, most of them are assigned to other cases, but every one of them keenly aware of this domestic terrorist....... the Specter, as the media likes to call him. They know that he has killed often and will likely kill again. I have asked my boss who leads the Criminal Investigation Division to have everyone keep all channels open throughout the various departments. The 'Vision' of the FBI is to 'stay ahead of the threat' and our 'Mission' is to 'protect the American people'. On both of those fronts right now we are failing. That is not acceptable. We have to catch this bastard. You have my contact information. Do not hesitate to call me."

Despite the gravity of the circumstances, Kim Holcomb had enjoyed her short time in Waukesha. It was good to get away from Minneapolis, to exchange ideas with fellow journalists, and to be romanced by the handsome Sam Proctor. It had been a whirlwind affair but in reality, with them living more than 300 miles apart, it would be one difficult to sustain and they both had busy careers to focus on. She had become something of a celebrity with her news breaking stories, and her good looks and articulate manner earned her several interviews from several local and even a few national TV stations on the scene. However, she had exhausted any further material to be gleaned from this killing and her editor was calling for her return to Minneapolis. He wanted her to do a deeper dive into the trail of the Specter's alleged killings and maybe develop a psychological profile. Granted, there had been no positive I.D., no notes found, no admission of guilt, but surely there was a story out there to be told about this ghost and maybe Kim's tagline in the news would invite someone to contact her. Kim made preparations to check out of her hotel and then run by the newspaper office to thank everyone for their accommodations. Lunch with Sam was the icing on the cake before she headed back home. It had been good to tip-toe back into a social life.

Wes guided the RV east out of Wisconsin towards Ohio while Marcia tidied up and quietly had the news on while she cleaned to learn of any breaking story. They had no timetable and no specific destination other than a quick return to Wes' hometown of Middleton, Ohio. For several years he had wisely been putting a little cash in his safety deposit box, knowing that if the day came that he would actually go off the grid, he had to maintain a very low electronic footprint. It was time to go back by his bank and reload. He knew all too well of the tremendous capabilities of the SuperComputer in Massachusetts used by the intelligence agencies. He was sure that the FBI had put together a profile of all of the sites of the killings and asked the computer if there was a common denominator, such as a credit or debit card that was used at each site. That search would likely have produced a list of one, and his name would have surfaced at the top.

CHAPTER 34

IT'S NOT ABOUT ME

WITH EACH PASSING day the trail grew colder. No witnesses, no further crime scene evidence and no mistakes by the killer. The investigation was hitting dead ends at every turn. The FBI decided to try and spur some interest by offering a $100K reward for any information but the announcement did little to spark any activity on the FBI hotline. When agent Raymond returned his team to D.C. they set up temporary headquarters for a task force in a warehouse in Georgetown. It offered plenty of space, seclusion, and privacy away from the press. Carpenters built rooms, technicians worked to install the latest gadgetry. Trucks hauled in rental furniture and the command center was stuffed with desks and chairs. A fleet of dark SUVs filled the parking lot and forty agents were assigned full time to the nationwide manhunt as well as a support staff. There was no budget. This was, after all, Washington D.C. and the suspect was a domestic terrorist who currently topped the FBI's Most Wanted List.

Kim Holcomb was back at her desk amid the clutter and the energy of the newsroom at the Minneapolis Star & Tribune.

Her star had ascended and she was given a little more latitude from her editor now as she continued to develop the story on the suspected trail of Specter. She was working the phones feverishly and balancing the calls with an avalanche of emails and texts. Her newspaper byline was synonymous with the Specter phenomenon, so of course she had to sort through all the crank calls and the kooks sending probing emails. Her editor had even assigned her a "stringer", or entry level reporter, to assist. In the midst of it all, one email on her laptop with the subject line *'It's not about me'* caught her eye. She was able to preview it without opening herself up to any virus and determined it was safe. She read:

My name is not important. What is important is that the string of retribution killings I have taken part in has very little to do with me and everything to do with a flawed justice system and corruption in our country that is out of control. I am not naive' enough to think that I alone can make a big difference. But I could no longer sit on the sidelines. If the American people can embrace the notion that there are consequences for one's actions and a reawakening of our citizens empowerment, maybe we can begin to reclaim our values - and our country. Thank you for your fair journalism. You tell the story, you stick to the facts, and you do not editorialize. This, regrettably, is a lost art in journalism. I appreciate you for telling a balanced story.

Specter

Kim sat back in her chair, rolled backward a moment to create some space and took a deep breath. After a moment she rolled forward again, read the email a second time, and decided to call Inspector Raymond. He was much easier to reach now that she had his cellphone number and she was evidently on his caller I.D. list. He answered on the third ring. "Good morning

Ms. Holcomb, how is stardom treating you"? She laughed off the question and explained to him what she had come across. He listened quietly, hesitated for a moment to digest it, and asked Kim to forward the email to him. He said he suspected it was sent from a burner phone but his team would learn what it could. He promised to keep her advised as it looked like this may be the first tangible lead if it was legit. She thanked him, hung up, and again eased back into her chair to give this some thought. Why not get involved in the most notorious FBI manhunt in the nation, she thought. If this was truly an email from Specter then he had selected her as his potential mouthpiece. She bent over her laptop and prepared a response, not even knowing if this so-called "burner phone" had the capability to receive messages.

Wes could have easily answered Kim's question for her. He could indeed receive responses to his emails and the activity could not be traced to his phone. He occasionally glanced at his screen to see if he had received an answer. He had debated whether or not to contact Kim in the first place. He wasn't looking for glory and certainly not for recognition. But he wanted to make sure that the message was clear that crime should not continue to be tolerated to the extent that it had. He and Marcia were enjoying a few days off the road in his Middleton, Ohio home and plotting a course that would eventually take them to the west coast. There were countless opportunities for criminal retribution along the way. With each day another gut wrenching story hit the news. But ultimately he wanted to go after "the big guy". The deviant who funded so many liberal causes with his billions and who was destroying the country. Wes had restocked the RV for departure in the morning and he and Marcia were enjoying a quiet winter evening in front of the fireplace catching up on the news. A story broke about a career criminal who had an argument with his girlfriend, the mother of his children, and burned her with lighter fluid over 60% of her body. Worse, she was pregnant with twins and in critical condition. After being arrested and charged, 41 year old Mr. Devonne Marsh posted a $5000 bond and walked out of jail. Wes was numb with anger. Angry at such inhumanity and angrier still at a system that allows anyone, much less a repeat offender, a get out of jail card. As he contemplated this he heard his phone ping. He checked the screen and was pleased to see that young Ms. Holcomb had answered his message. He smiled and handed his phone to Marcia who read it herself and said "it looks like you have a new friend".

CHAPTER 35

THE MIDWAY

THEIR OBJECTIVE WAS to head west, and so they would. But Detroit was in fact about four hours north of them and Wes and Marcia weighed the deviation from their plan against the senselessness of the crime. It did not take them long to agree that Mr. Devonne Marsh deserved a visit. They finished their coffee and rolled out of the driveway headed due north on I-75. Traffic was fairly heavy and slow but they were in no hurry and Wes stopped frequently to stretch his legs and watch behind him. He was aware that as the allure of the Specter increased, so too would the heat from the Feds. He found himself spending nearly as much time looking in the rearview mirror as he did watching the road ahead. When they stopped for a meal he always made sure he got a table with a view of the parking lot. If they happened to go into a store he would nonchalantly find cover and watch the front door while Marcia shopped. It didn't take long for her to pick up on his paranoia. As they resumed their trip Marcia glanced over at him, held his hand and said "Are you worried about us getting caught?" Wes was caught off guard and was not aware that she had picked up on his changed behavior. He should have known better. "I am happier than I have been in a long time", he said. "I love every mile that we log together, I have plenty of cash, a beautiful woman beside me and I'm finally able to do something meaningful to me. I am drowning in freedom but I want to make sure that I don't lose it." Marcia settled back to absorb those comments and decided that she liked them. "But you didn't answer my question, are you worried?". "No", he replied, "not worried, only cautious. There is too much at stake here and our freedom just might be the least of the concerns." She understood and settled back into thought as they continued north. In a couple of hours they reached Toledo.

Marcia had done a search for a good internet cafe in Toledo and they decided on "The Midway" on Lincoln Ave. The menu offered good soup and sandwiches, it was easy enough to reach from the interstate, and touted ample parking for oversized vehicles. Her GPS brought them right to the spot. Wes settled the RV into the lot and went in to select a table where they could watch the parking lot.

Once they had settled in and ordered a couple of grilled Chicken Caesar wraps, Wes used his prepaid credit card from Walgreens and used the cafe's server to browse the internet. He accessed a back channel that law enforcement officials often used. He wanted to learn everything he could about Mr. Devonne Marsh. As a repeat criminal offender, a parolee, and out on bail pending a trial hearing, he was not at all surprised that Mr. Marsh was outfitted with the latest rage in convict's fashion. He wore a SCRAM, the most widely used ankle monitoring bracelet in the corrections industry. It continuously tracked him 24/7 in real time and reported to authorities if he was in an excluded area. It also monitored perspiration through pores and if a con was drinking alcohol it was metabolized and emitted as sweat. In other words, Mr. Marsh could not run, he could not hide. Wes cleared a secondary level of security on the law enforcement tab and learned that his culprit lived in the Detroit neighborhood of Brush Park. Brush Park deserved further research. Wes learned that it held the dubious distinction of being the second worst neighborhood in the city. It rated 7097 violent crimes per 100,000 people - a rate that was 250% higher than inner city Detroit itself. He snapped an internet photo of the "perp" and ended his search. He and Marcia enjoyed their wraps, paid their tab and hopped back on I-75 towards Detroit. Greenfield RV Park lay on the western fringe of Detroit, strategically close to the blighted Brush Park neighborhood. Wes and Marcia arrived well before dark and requested a quiet spot at the back of the property. Wes paid cash for a 3-night stay at $28 per night and they settled in to develop a plan on how to pay a visit to Mr. Marsh.

CHAPTER 36

BRUSHPARK

IT WAS LITTLE MORE than a ten minute drive from the RV site to Brush Park, but Wes had decided to leave the RV in place and rent a car for the three days that he and Marcia planned to be in the Detroit area. Not only was it more nimble, but a lot less noticeable, as an RV would look out of place in the blighted Brush Park Neighborhood. The Brush Park historic district is a 22-block neighborhood located completely within midtown Detroit. Wes decided to play it safe and leave Marcia behind. He made the short drive southwest down Fisher Freeway, punching radio buttons to find some soothing music. Every station was preprogrammed to rap music so he manually rotated the dial until he found a little Kenny Chesney. Soon he turned left onto Polk St. where Mr. Devonne Marsh was last reported to be living with his cousin Ladarius Stiles. Stiles was a neighborhood gang banger with a rap sheet and it was not hard to locate his house. Marsh was required to physically check in with his case officer each week. As Wes drove slowly through the neighborhood to get a sense of the layout, he felt sad at the obvious decline of what was a once proud area. Late

Victorian and French Renaissance Revival style architectural homes still dotted the landscape but all were in disrepair and many were abandoned. His research of Detroit had told him that there were as many as 70,000 abandoned buildings in the city and it had seen its population fall from 1,850,000 to 650,000 in just a few short decades.

The urban decay was severe and it was everywhere. He kept a low profile and slunk deep into his seat of the dark Ford Taurus. He was armed and on high alert but nonetheless did not feel safe. This was just one example of so many inner city slums across our nation where the young boys are getting high at 15, getting hooked at 16 and running drugs to support their habit. The girls get pregnant at 16. Kids having kids. Babies that nobody wants. Students bussed an hour away to schools out of the district where they didn't fit in made it easy for guys like Marsh to quit and return to the streets. No job skills to offer, and little chance for opportunity with a poor command of the English language and no father figure for guidance. Wes had an epiphany as he drove the filthy streets. He suddenly felt a little sorry for the Devonne Marshs' of the world. They were unwitting victims of their environment and of a collapse of an entire demographic set. And yet, there had to be consequences for his hideous actions. He was after all an adult and knew right from wrong. At that moment Wes decided he would spare his life but would apply the "eye for an eye" punishment.

Mr. Johnny Sample was Devonne's case officer and maintained an office on Mack St. several blocks off of Fisher Freeway. He had received a call in his office earlier that day from Wes, under an assumed name, who had identified himself as a crime reporter for the Gannet New Organization and said that he was developing a story on crime trends and how they affect communities and every day people. He said he was particularly interested in the challenges of the Brush Park area and had a love for telling the stories that no one else was telling. Over the course of the casual conversation Wes gained the confidence of Mr. Sample and learned that Devonne was required to visit his office each Monday, late morning to describe what his weekend was like. Once he learned that Marsh was staying with his cousin on Polk Street, Wes thanked Mr. Sample for his insight into neighborhood crime and promised to keep him informed on his progress. It was Friday afternoon and Wes drove the route from Mr. Sample's office to the cousin's house several times, identifying the best place for an intercept and an unimpeded exit. Given the number of abandoned houses, it was not hard to develop a strategy, and he even spotted Marsh and a few fellow thugs hanging at the corner of Polk and Harris Street smoking cigarettes. He kept his ballcap pulled low, turned his country music down and avoided eye contact but there was no mistaking Marsh from his mug shot. Having satisfied himself with his thorough reconnaissance, Wes jumped on the Freeway and headed back to Marcia.

He entered the RV to find her stretched out on the couch and catching up on both the local and national news. "Nothing new to report" she said as Wes sidled over and gave her a big hug and kiss. "I'm famished", she said, "and I've been doing a little homework of my own. What would you say to a nice Mediterranean dinner tonight - my treat"? "How could I turn that down, love me some Mediterranean food - whatcha got"? Marcia told him that she found a highly rated place with the freshest fattoush in town and a great wine list to boot. Wes begged for a ten minute reprieve to shower away the grime of the slum city and said he would fill her in on what he saw today over dinner.

Malek Al Kabob was everything the internet promised. The spacious restaurant offered earth toned walls of tan and brown, ornate carpet and heavy wooden furniture. They were courteously escorted to a table for two and Wes sat with his back to the wall and his eyes on the door. Marcia smiled in acceptance and asked for a wine list. She ordered a Shawaram Plate of half lamb, half chicken and a Greek Salad. Wes stuck with the Fattoush and ordered a side dish of Chicken Saggi. Once the order was taken Marcia ordered a 2014 Sokos Central Greece Savatiano while Wes could only shake his head in appreciation. He thought of himself as something of a "foodie" but was quickly learning that he played second fiddle to his well traveled culinary companion. Over a delicious and leisurely dinner Wes told Marcia about his scouting trip and his plan for next Monday morning. She was disappointed to learn that he would go solo on this one but he was insistent that he wasn't going to parade some "hottie" around in the ghetto. The night unfolded pleasantly for the couple as the meal was finished with a house frozen custard and an Ouzo. They could not have known that their return to the RV would put a damper on the entire evening.

CHAPTER 37

FATHERLESS CHILDREN

UPON RETURNING to their RV later that evening, Wes & Marcia kicked off their shoes, popped the cork on a nice bottle of Chenin Blanc, and settled into the couch to catch up on the latest. News of the local weather confirmed it was time to get out of Detroit and head south for the winter. National news followed with recycled stories of the stalled economy, inflation running amok and soaring gas prices. The talking heads reported that the current President's poll numbers were well under water and continuing to sag further, making him the least respected President ever. The Dems were sweating the next elections and a number of Democratic incumbents feared losing their jobs aboard the party's sinking ship. Finally the news switched to a breaking story of out of Texas where a man reportedly pumped 22 rounds into his girlfriend in a fit or rage and left her dead. The macabre part of the story was that he was already out on parole and within days of his release some "do gooder" had gotten to him and emptied an entire gun clip into him. The reporter on the scene speculated on whether or not this was yet another act of The Specter. Reportedly, the

FBI was on the scene aiding local law enforcement. Wes sat there taking it all in and was stunned, while Marica seemed to be elated. "Praise God" she proclaimed, while Wes looked on in astonishment. "Don't you see what this can do to us"? he asked her. "We can be linked to any random killing out there, whether justified or not. These are the unintended consequences for our actions that maybe I should have foreseen. He lapsed into quiet thought and they finished their wine and went to bed. But for Wes sleep was fleeting and in fact so elusive and so fitful that he wasn't sure he slept at all.

The couple decided to avoid all news the next morning and make the most of their short stay in the area. After coffee and toast they drove to nearby Greenfield Village in Dearborn to visit the highly acclaimed Henry Ford Museum of American Innovation. This was the home of Industrial development and proudly exhibited of the spirit of Americana. Wes would normally have been in awe of this historical presentation but his thoughts were elsewhere. Nonetheless he soldiered through it, as Marcia was enjoying the tour, and by early afternoon they were tired and famished. They made their way downtown to a Greek neighborhood diner where Marcia opted for Spanokopita and Wes enjoyed the house renowned trio of meats dish. Dessert was pistachio Baklava and, feeling sufficiently bloated, it was time to return to the RV. Wes was quieter than usual on the trip home and finally Marcia asked what was eating at him. He told her about his epiphany the day before and how while punks like Devonne Marsh cruelly left hapless victims in their wake, they themselves were victims of a flawed societal breakdown. He spoke of a recent interview he had watched on Fox News with Rightwing U.S. Pundit and Political Commentator Candace Owens. He said she often referred to the "fatherless children" in the African American communities and how it was tearing the fabric of those communities apart all across the nation. He expressed admiration for her tough stance, knowing that it opened her up to criticism from both the left and the RINOs (Republican in name only) on the right. One side labeled her as an "Uncle Tom", while the other, of course, threw out their favorite word "racist", said Wes. "Well,", he opined, "it's been said that real leaders never walk down the middle, and this is a good illustration. She has the courage of her convictions and my admiration". They made the rest of the trip home in silence; Wes pondering his next move and Marcia wondering if he was having a change of heart and would be able to see this whole thing through to its conclusion; whatever "through" happened to be.

Sunday morning broke clear, crisp and, for Wes, with a renewed sense of purpose. He had determined overnight that he wanted to distance himself from any vigilante activity and make it clear that he was not endorsing this behavior. He was up early and quietly made a pot of coffee while allowing Marcia to sleep in. He pulled out a new burner phone and composed an email to Kim Holcomb at the Minneapolis Star disavowing his alleged involvement in the Texas murder. He said that he recognized the hypocrisy of his words, but hoped that people would understand that there still has to be account-ability for one's actions; a notion which we as a nation seem to have allowed to go by the wayside. He closed his email by again thanking Kim for her unbiased reporting and wished her a kinder and gentler world.

CHAPTER 38

UP IN SMOKE

IT WAS PRECISELY 10:30 a.m. when Wes glanced at his watch as he sat quietly in his Taurus, neatly tucked into the shade of an abandoned building on Polk Street. He had selected this spot because it was obscure, offered a good view of the street, and was directly on the route that Devonne Marsh should be taking any moment. His appointment with his P.O. was at 10:00 on Mondays and never lasted more than a half hour. For now all was quiet, but Wes knew that he couldn't count on that luck to hold out too long. Timing was everything and he needed Marsh to be smoking a cigarette and have nobody else on the street. Moments later he saw the silhouette of Marsh making its way along Polk towards him while still more than a block away. There was nobody else in sight but Marsh had not yet lit a cigarette. Soon however Wes saw him shake one from its pack, place it between his lips and strike a match as he continued to walk towards Wes' car. When he saw the glow of the lit cigarette, Wes started his engine, put it in drive, and slowly made his way towards the figure. He glanced left and right as he cautiously approached Mr. Marsh. When he was within ten yards of him he slowed even more, stuck his head out of the window and asked "can you tell me where the nearest gas station is"? Marsh slowed as he considered the question but had no time to answer or even be suspicious. Wes pointed his aerosol can of a mixed acetone and kerosene accelerant right at the convict's face and sprayed. It had the effect of a mini flame thrower as it hit the lit cigarette and a small explosion occurred covering Marsh's upper torso in flames. Hearing the screams as he pulled away, he looked once again to insure there were no witnesses. He didn't see any so he obeyed the speed limit and made a right hand turn off of Polk and onto Hwy. 81, headed northeast towards the RV campground. Wes, of course, had no idea that Mr. Chase Ellis sat on his front porch that morning, as he did most mornings, idly watching the street. He had a front row seat as the crime scene unfolded and was quick to call 911. His reaction likely spared the life of Devonne Marsh, but not before significantly burning his body. He rolled in the grass mostly out of instinct to quell the flames but his charred torso would be an appropriate bookend to that of his girlfriend who at that very moment was on life support in the burn ward of Detroit Medical. Investigators on the scene learned that the "perp" was a white male in a dark, late model Ford. Nothing more could be determined however.

Wes and Marcia had readied the RV for departure that morning. Wes drove straight to the campground where Marcia assumed control of the car and Wes followed her to the car rental agency. They returned the vehicle without incident and minutes later were headed south on Interstate 75 towards Indiana where they planned to spend the night. As he waited for the traffic to open up a little on the outskirts of the city, Wes relayed to Marcia how the incident had played out and how Mr. Devonne Marsh was now sufficiently paid back for torching his pregnant girlfriend. He told the story with no sense of satisfaction whatsoever. In fact he found himself once again wrestling with his conscience on meting out punishment for those who had not been appropriately dealt with for their crime. And yet he consoled himself with the hope that maybe these lessons would send a strong enough message and make some crooks think twice about taking innocent victims. Even if it only means one or two people are spared a horrible fate, perhaps that makes it worth it, thought Wes. He focused on the road and the trip ahead and decided to let everything else run its course.

At noon FBI Special Investigator Mark Raymond stood over a conference phone with his two underlings on either side. The large meeting table in his makeshift office was ringed with chairs but nobody sat. Mark spoke into the phone. "Kim, thank you again for calling me back and I apologize for your wait. I now have my Assistant Deputy Director, Ryan Young, and my Communications Director, Cathy Milhoan with me to hear from you first hand before we develop a response strategy. I appreciate you forwarding to me the message from the so-called Specter. As we expected it was untraceable and was likely sent from a burner phone with prepaid minutes. The essence of the message is that Specter denies any involvement in the recent killing in Texas, despite it having a similar MO to his other hits. He also asks that you use your resources through the news-paper to denounce random killings from angered citizens. Is that the way you understand it?" Kim tingled with excitement at this new development and responded affirmatively. Raymond asked if she had answered him yet, to which she said no, not yet. She said that she wanted to share this with him first but she did want to follow up as well as expand on her story. Mark said he was grateful and asked that she hold off until she heard back from them. He promised to do so within twenty four hours and asked, in closing, if she had heard anything else from him and if she had any certainty that these emails were in fact coming from Specter. Kim answered that she had heard nothing else and had no way of knowing if this was the real culprit, but her instincts told her that it was. The team thanked Kim and said it would be in touch.

Once Mark Raymond cut the connection, Cathy Milhoan spoke up. She said that her analytics team had read both messages numerous times and the style was the same, suggesting only that it was likely the same sender but not necessarily Specter himself. Ryan Young added that if they acted upon the assumption that this was Specter and that Kim had his ear, maybe it was time to talk about offering a plea deal. Maybe they could quietly grant him witness protection and hide him to stop the killings and get the monkey off the back of the FBI, he said. Nobody really liked this idea as it was essentially a cover up. But they had run into dead ends with every crime and they were even further stung by the breaking news that morning of another incident in Detroit that had all the earmarks of Specter. A precision strike of a convicted felon who had gotten off light and with nobody to I.D. the attacker. It did not look good for America's leading law enforcement agency.

SOUTHBOUND

NEWS of the torching in Detroit that morning raced across the media platforms like a windblown brushfire. This had all the earmarks of one of those delicious breaking news stories that the public just lapped up. This story would captivate readers and viewers with the likes of the Casey Anthony story, Jon Benet Ramsey, Jodi Arias and even a little O.J. Simpson thrown in. A punk criminal torches his pregnant girlfriend in a fit of rage then gets himself torched in return. Even better, it had every indication that the Specter was once again at work performing heroic deeds and seeking retribution while law enforcement agencies shuffled paperwork. What a delicious tidbit for all the news agencies, and they ran with it - hard. Kim Holcomb was at her desk in the Minneapolis Star & Tribune newsroom when the story crossed the wire. She decided to take matters into her own hands. She pulled out her phone and responded to the last message she had received from Specter. She asked if he had been responsible for the Detroit attack and if he could prove so. She wanted to be certain that she was dealing with the actual Specter. Then she put her cell phone aside and called Mark Raymond from her land line. He answered on the third ring with "let me guess, you decided to contact your perp to see if he is responsible for the attack in Detroit today". After a slight hesitation she answered "I should have known I couldn't get ahead you, and yes, I did send a message and wanted you to be the first to know. I have a great public interest story on this guy which grows by the week and I can't lose steam on it". "I don't blame you", was Raymond's response, "just keep me in the loop on anything you get". "I promise", she said and hung up.

It has often been said that for every action, there is an equal and opposite reaction. And so it was with this latest media hysteria about Specter. While jubilant soccer moms, hotel maids and Starbuck barristers took to the streets with signs proclaiming Specter as Savior, regrettably others followed his lead by taking the law into their own hands. Reports on what were being called "revenge killings" across the nation had increased nearly tenfold. Do-gooders, inspired by Specter's actions, suddenly felt empowered to act. They had seen years of police defunding and a liberal court system which put crooks back on the streets with no bail. It was time to take matters into their own hands, they reasoned, if those who were paid to do so would not.

The FBI was keenly aware of this vengeance movement, and deeply concerned. Its makeshift command center in the warehouse in suburban Maryland now really did take on the aura of a War Room and had been provided with all the latest visual data. You could look at any city in the world by hacking into traffic cameras and security surveillance. Analysts received military radar in real time and you could pick up any television station in the world. There was just no getting around all of the latest electronic gadgetry available to the world's top crime fighting agency. They held all the marbles, and yet one man managed to dodge them at every turn. Special Investigator Raymond and his team were getting no closer to Specter. He slipped into, and presumably out of, Detroit without so much as a footprint. He managed to take out yet another high profile perp and the team began second guessing itself and wondering if it should have seen this one coming. Their crime analysts tried to categorize other likely targets but the list seemed endless. FBI headquarters was calling for results and those calls were very poignant. The FBI Director was under heavy scrutiny from Washington and things looked bad for an agency with 35,000 men and women on the payroll who were presently befuddled by the actions of a single culprit.

Meanwhile Wes was thoroughly enjoying his own command post at the helm of his very cozy RV Coach as he comfortably navigated it south down I-65 through the cornfields of southern Indiana. He glanced to his right and was pleased to see that Marcia was soundly asleep, tucked comfortably beneath a blanket in the passenger seat. He realized at that very moment that he was on this journey because of people just like Marcia. He knew that he was falling in love with her and warmly embraced that emotion. It had dawned on him the other day as he shaved that the masculine smell of Old Spice in his bathroom had given way to more genteel fragrances of women's body perfume. He was in a committed relationship and he loved it. He would do anything to protect her. He believed with all his heart in freedom, democracy and justice. But those values were under attack, all over the world, and people, like Marcia, were merely the victims in a world gone mad. He resolved to do everything within his power to draw his own line in the sand and say "enough". Whatever the cost.

CHAPTER 40

LET'S TALK

IF NOTHING ELSE, Kim was an extremely disciplined person when it came to her personal fitness regimen. Therefore, when her alarm clock shook her out of a deep slumber at 5:00 a.m. that morning, she dutifully rolled out of bed, pulled on her workout togs, laced up her Nikes and went to the bathroom to splash some water on her face. She swallowed a cup of coffee on the way over to her 24/7 fitness center and swiped her key fob to gain entry. It was still pitch dark outside but the overhead banks of fluorescents had the workout room well lit. By 5:30 she was pounding the Peloton across the hills of the San Fernando Valley on the video screen while scrolling through her emails from the night before. Much of it was the usual nonsensical spam and more than a few random emails from admirers who had learned to navigate the system and had signed on to her account. Since her revelation of the Specter in her column in the Minneapolis newspaper she had become a popular correspondent. Nonetheless, most of it was clutter until she came across one with the subject matter of "let's talk". That intrigued her and she opened it to read further. Sure enough, it was purportedly from the Specter himself who wanted to have a confidential conversation with her. He was aware of her charge to create a story on him and he wanted the record to be accurate. He asked when a convenient time would be so they could talk without interference.

Kim was nearing the end of her punishing 30 minute cardio session over the California mountains and slowed her pace and until her heartbeat returned to normal. When she finished her cool down session she wiped down the peloton with a sanitized wipe, rehydrated, and went to work on the weight machines. It was Tuesday which meant upper torso strength training. Thursday's workout would focus on lower body muscles followed by a blend of the two parts of the anatomy on Saturday. Each session always began with a cardio warmup. Kim had a killer body for a reason - she earned it. As she sipped some power fuel she composed a thoughtful response in her mind to Specter's question. She stepped off the quad extension machine, closely followed by the appreciative eyes of a few testosterone loaded steroid junkies. She was used to this and deflected attention by keeping her earpods firmly implanted and smiling politely but dismissively when someone entered her aura. They usually lost interest quickly and returned to flexing in front of the mirrors. She punched in a response to Specter on her phone and suggested that she would be in the office later that morning and available after an early morning strategy meeting with the news staff. She provided him with her land line number and asked if he could call her at around 10:00. She received a positive response from him momentarily with the caveat that it would only be the two of them having that conversation. She assured him that it would be.

Wes and Marcia were absolutely enjoying the freedom of the open road once again, perched high in their seats in the RV overlooking the landscape of central Kentucky. They had briefly overnighted at a truck stop in southern Indiana before getting on the road once again early in the morning. The gently rolling hills along I-65 which defined the bluegrass region of the state was known for its bourbon and thoroughbred horses. However tobacco was still the main cash crop and acres and acres of it lay to the east and west of the interstate as they headed south. Wes spied a Stuckeys sign indicating that one of its outlets was only a few miles ahead. It would be a good chance to stop and fuel up he thought and grab one of those renowned pecan log rolls that he always favored as a kid while on road trips with his parents. He expertly wheeled the RV into a space by a diesel fuel pump and began topping off his tank. Marcia headed into the shop to hit the restroom and Wes asked her to grab him a pecan log. She returned in a matter of minutes with the pecan log and a smile that could not be contained. "I bought you a present" she said, and handed him a coffee mug. Wes beamed as he looked at the white porcelain cup which said "May the Specter be with you" and had a silhouette of a darkened looming figure in the background wielding a pistol. "God bless the indomitable spirit of the American entrepreneur", said Wes and shook his head in disbelief. "I found it right beside the "Let's go Brandon" cups chuckled Marcia.

CHAPTER 41

HAYSTACK

WES PULLED the RV into a rest stop along I-65 as the 10:00 a.m. hour approached. While Marcia headed for the restroom, he pulled out a burner phone with prepaid minutes and dialed the number that Kim Holcomb had given him. She answered on the second ring. He allowed her to ask a few questions to confirm that he was in fact her "Specter" and then took the lead. He and Marcia had a long discussion the night before and decided that because of his actions, others were following suit and those unintended consequences could potentially spin out of control. He did not want that responsibility and therefore was going to cease his criminal manhunts. He told Kim of his intentions, knowing that she would appreciate it was the right thing to do. He asked her to consider composing a final piece to conclude the story of Specter and he would not be heard from again. He hung up and crushed the phone with the heel of his boot, then discarded it in a nearby trash bin.

Wes placed a second call on another burner phone to an old buddy in McAllen, Texas. Haskell "Haystack" Calhoun was a giant of a man who Wes had gone through some specialized police training courses with a few years ago. They had instantly bonded. So much so that they had remained friends over the years and had even taken a few vacations together in the great outdoors. Most memorable of those was a trout fishing trip on the Klamath River in Oregon where Wes landed the biggest trout he had ever seen. As he and Haystack stoked the fire that evening and heated the cast iron skillet in preparation for the meal, a large black bear roamed out of the Oregon wilderness towards them with ideas of claiming that fish for himself. Wes froze when he heard the growl but Haystack rose to his full six foot seven inch, 290 pound size, armed himself with that iron skillet, and let out a yell that must surely have been heard back in Portland. The bear turned tail, never looked back, and Wes and Haystack enjoyed a lighter moment, armed with a story that was of course embellished every time they told it. Wes was able to reach his friend through the border patrol switchboard after identifying himself. He was patched through to McAllen office from which Haystack oversaw three counties stretching more than 120 miles of the Tex-Mex border. He sounded genuinely thrilled to hear from Wes and they arranged to meet late the next afternoon at a remote landing strip twelve miles outside of McAllen at a detention center.

The de Haviland Twin Otter turbo prop approached the landing strip so slowly that it appeared to be hovering. Although her design dated back to the mid-60s, the high-winged aircraft continued to be a favorite among bush pilots the world over. She could land on just about a thousand feet of surface and take off in even less. This aircraft was made to handle the hard pan of the desert and a landing strip had been marked with orange flags adjacent to the dilapidated, rusting metal detention building. The pilot nimbly set the plane down in a whirl of dust. The blast of her turboprops kicked up even more dirt when she slowed and she was enveloped momentarily in a cloud. Power was taken off the props and when dust settled Haskell "Haystack" Calhoun uncorked his massive frame from the aircraft. For a man of nearly 300 pounds, he proved surprisingly agile as he grabbed the strut and swung to the ground. Wes shook his head in admiration, waited for his buddy to shake some of dust off himself, slap his cowboy hat against his leg to rid it of the red river dust and strode over to Wes, squeezing him with a big bear hug. "Little buddy, it has been way too long. So good to see you, what brings you down to my part of the world." "Plenty of time to catch up on all that pal, first of all let me introduce you to my girlfriend Marcia". Haystack lumbered over, removed his hat and extended his hand to Marcia which completely wrapped his giant meathook around most of her lower arm. He smiled at her with genuinely warm, cobalt blue eyes and studied her like a jeweler studies a diamond. "Little lady, I am so glad to meet you. Let's all go somewhere so that we can wash down some of this desert dust and I'll tell you some stories about this guy you are hanging out with that may change your mind."

CHAPTER 42

THE FLIES

AFTER A QUICK BREAKFAST of coffee and bagels, Wes and Haystack left Marcia to get settled into the house, unpack some of her belongings and allow herself to primp for the day. After all, a girl can only go so long without plucking, polishing and primping. It was "girl day" and everyone was happy with her decision to remain behind. They hopped in the Bronco and headed west towards the desert detention facility when a static laced message came over Haystack's radio. He was alerted of a "situation" about forty minutes from his location by one of his agents in the field. "Hang on buddy," he said to Wes, "you're about to see the ugly side of this job". Their trip across the desert provided a long, flat vista of sand, rock, and a few dried up pale yellow scrub bushes. Everything looked to be some shade of tan and was as bleak the moonscape. Far to the south Wes saw the raw mountains of Mexico. Up ahead to the west were the desperate little baked terra cotta towns that dotted the border land. Border security knew that many of these were used as waystations for trafficking. After nearly an hour on unimproved road, the truck crossed into Zapata County and reached a few meager adobe homes where agents were waiting. The homes looked like they leaned on each other to stay upright. Haystack and

Wes followed an agent into the first of them. The five dead bodies lay bloated inside their clothes. The smell of poverty and rot was the same the world over and Haystack pulled a handkerchief over his nose and handed a second one to Wes. The flies. Damn! All Wes could do was stare at the bodies and wonder where the hell the flies had come from and how they had gotten here so quickly. They were out in full force despite the bodies looking to be less than a few days old. Flies were landing on sunken eyeballs and laying their eggs on openings in the nostrils and mouths. These wretched souls had no I.D. on them and had probably tried multiple crossings before only to be caught and deported back to Mexico again and again. This one proved to be their fatal final attempt. They probably wanted nothing more than a fruit picker's job in Sacramento or a dishwasher's job at Applebee's to support their infant children back home. And sadly, here they lay, their mission failed as people milled around the corpses seemingly unfazed. They had seen it all before. One onlooker observed that this happened all the time. "You watch, no one will remember him tomorrow" he said in halting English. There was conviction in his words.

Agents were trying to get positive identification on them with fingerprints and DNA samples and cross reference them against the national database. More often that not it a futile effort. The M.O. here had all the earmarks of a coyote charging these "John Does" a fee to get them across the border and then abandoning them. There were no wound marks, however tracks tracing out for many miles in each direction indicated that they had probably searched for days for a way out in vain. Left with no food, water or a map, they never had much chance. Haystack had his men photograph and tag the bodies and called in a helicopter transport to take them to McAllen for a quick autopsy.

CHAPTER 43

DESPERATE PEOPLE

ON THE RIDE back east Wes sat numbed by the experience. Haystack had seen it too many times before but it never really got easier. He broke the silence after a while. "There's days I'm in favor of giving this whole damn place back to 'em", he said, staring out the window straight ahead. "You sign on for the ride and you probably think you know where the ride is going. Turns out to be a little rougher than you had in mind. Probably nobody would blame me if I quit. But I can't do that. This is my home, this is what I am. I can't pass this along to anyone else. I'll probably be here 'til hell freezes over, and then stay a while longer on the ice." He continued to stare straight ahead as he drove in silence. He couldn't name the feeling. He was empty. It was nearly defeat.

Wes and Haystack pulled the Land Rover over to a widened spot along the dusty desert road and stepped out. They immediately began swatting flies as they scanned the horizon with binoculars looking for the next group of desperate people seeking to breach America's defenses. They had spent a few moments that sweltering morning talking with other migrants at the way station who had paid their last dollars that they could scrape together to pay a "coyote" to help them navigate through the desert and across the border. And then they were abandoned as quickly as they had arrived to make their own way. Hundreds died every year but that wasn't enough to deter them from trying. They were easy for Border Patrol Agents to spot; dark t-shirts with powdery salt rings under the armpits and circling the neck. Sneakers that looked like they'd been through a meat grinder. Dusty backpacks with extra socks and a few cans of food. Refried beans, jugs of water and garlic, always fresh garlic. It was believed that mosquitos didn't like human flesh that smelled of garlic or that , God forbid, if they died in the desert scavengers would not feed on garlic infused human remains. Wes' heart ached for these browned, sweating bodies bent with exhaustion and faces etched with weariness and fear. And now as he and Haystack looked out across the vast expanse of the desert terrain, they awaited the next movement which, according the the captured migrants, would soon come. Wes marveled that in spite of all this hardship, the beauty of the desert could be overwhelming. It can make you forget how cruel and unforgiving this terrain can be for those caught in its clutches in the summer.

After a while Haystack tried to break the silence by turning the radio on. He navigated the entire bandwidth without anything more than static. "Not even any Mexican music", he said. "Where else in the country can you go and not have access to a single radio station?". There was a hint of whimsy in his voice and Wes smiled at the attempt of humor. "At least there wasn't any rap music", he said. They both chuckled and continued to watch the desert dust blow by. Wes did not consider himself a religious man, but he was spiritual and he felt at that moment that maybe God had placed him here for a reason. He knew that his conscience would move him to get involved and he needed to decide what that would entail. And what to do about Marcia. He was grateful that she had decided not to ride along with them that day.

CHAPTER 44

NO RETREAT

WHEN DEATH APPROACHES in the desert there are few places to hide. There are no giant oaks or cool elms to seek refuge under, just spindly cacti. If one can find shade in a hurry it's a luxury and only lasts as long as the sun sits still. By noon the sun is staring directly down upon you and to protect yourself you end up having to jump from shadow to shadow in a leap frog manner towards freedom. Border crossers on the verge of death often huddle under trees only to be found dead later after being rotisserie cooked by the rotating sun. A carcass left out in the open becomes a miniature laboratory. Flies buzz around, ants crawl on the skin, maggots shuffle in the openings and gases build up within the body cavity and are then expelled. It is a grotesque sight but uncommonly real for those who fail to make it safely across the border to shelter. Wes and Haystack scanned the horizon with binoculars looking for turkey vultures which circle the skies seeking carcasses in the state of decay. It was a gruesome task but one which has an end game. Find the migrants and backtrack to the coyote who placed them in this vulnerable situation. The Border Patrol's fight was no so much with the illegals, for who could fault them, as it was with those who capitalized on them and then left them to die. The ruthless coyotes, the drug smugglers, the human traffickers and the terrorists. That was the end game.

After nearly eight hours in the unrelenting sun, and with no sign of activity, Wes and Haystack returned to a migrant encampment to question a few recent captives. An old man is lying on a bunk in the shelter staring blankly at the ceiling. He ignores them and they come in. His wife died in the desert and they had to leave her body behind. They just covered her up and left her. He is in shock and remains mute for the entire evening. Two shelter workers take him by the arms and escort him to the kitchen. His feet barely leave the ground as he shuffles down the hall. He sits quietly for twenty minutes and stares a bowl of beans before being escorted back to his bed. There is nothing left to say. Wes and Haystack realize the futility of trying to get any information out of him and decide to return to McAllen.

CHAPTER 45

MCALLEN, TX

AS THEY ROLLED BACK across the desert towards town, Haystack felt that they had dealt with enough for one day and decided to take the rest of the day off and show his guests the good side of McAllen, Texas. He called the Medical Examiner at McAllen General Hospital to alert him of the arrival of the bodies and to confirm his suspicion that cause of death was dehydration. Then he and Wes drove across town to his ranch home to pick up Marcia. She came out to meet them in the driveway and appeared properly scrubbed and fluffed and looked amazing as she sashayed out in her skin-tight designer jeans, her mid-calf cowgirl boots and a snug top that left nothing to imagine on her curvaceous figure. Haystack stepped out of the Bronco with his hands on his hips, removed his cowboy hat and sunglasses, ran his hand through his thin, sandy hair and just stared in admiration. "Honey, I was figuring on takin' you into town today but we may need an armed guard. McAllen don't often see the likes of you", he said. As usual, Marcia blushed and gratefully accepted the compliments. She smiled, spun around on her heels so the boys could enjoy the full effect, and then pronounced that she was starving and wanted to try out some of the McAllen cuisine for lunch.

The three of them drove towards downtown as Haystack gave them a brief bio of the city. It was located at the southern tip of the state in the Rio Grande Valley and was largely agricultural. Despite being a border town, said Haystack, it had a vibrant metro area, a high quality of life, and a young bicultural community. The city sat across the border from Reynoso, Mexico and between the two metropolises there was a population of almost 1.5 million. Cross border trading between the two nations made McAllen a good place live and to retire, he proudly stated. Haystack headed directly to the "Cowboy Chicken", his proclaimed favorite lunch stop. They nabbed a table on the outdoor patio, after the usual round of friendly greetings, and Haystack insisted that they try the wood fired rotisserie chicken with mac & cheese and okra and ranch beans on the side. He got no argument.

As they waited for their food, Marcia steered the conversation to a serious matter that she had been reading about that morning. It was an article about the millions of enslaved people worldwide and it had called special attention to Mexico City which reportedly had an estimated 18,000 enslaved. Of those, she said, one in three was a child and there were no existing social services to help. She continued that this population knew nothing but poverty, hunger and sexual abuse. Young girls made up the largest demographic but also young boys, transgenders and even the disabled she said and she was heartbroken after reading the story. She could barely contain her grief as she voiced her disgust at how there could be such a worldwide appetite for this perversion. The story reported it to be a multi-billion dollar industry which bought off government and law enforcement officials, allowing sex traffickers to sell off children to the highest bidders, she said. She apologized for casting such a dark mood over the afternoon but felt moved to do something. Without revealing all the grim details of his morning, Wes told her what they discovered earlier that day and said that he too was moved to help. At that moment the two of them realized the course of their lives had changed dramatically

CHAPTER 46

THE BORDER

HAYSTACK CALHOUN PICKED up the two Dos Equis beers off the bar, paid the tab, and turned back to the table, ignoring the fact that the bartender seemed to recoil at his presence. He had seen it all before and knew that in his position with Border Enforcement many people just recognized him as a threat and preferred to keep their distance. He returned to the small table against the wall where Wes waited and placed the beers, dripping with cold moisture, in front of him. Haystack tossed his bottle back taking in half the beer with the first gulp and savored the sensation of the cold brew hitting the back of his throat. He placed the half empty bottle back on the table and said "Mexican border, Mexican beer", ceremoniously wiping his mouth with his shirt sleeve. "Seriously", answered Wes, "they don't have any good American beers here?". Haystack calmly smiled and explained that the choice of beer was a side signal to his few informants who frequented the bar and let them know that he had not been tailed here. Had he chosen any other brand it would have been a signal to not approach. Now it was just a matter of time, sitting back in the air conditioning, slaking their thirst from another dusty day in the desert, and seeing if anyone would come around with some good poop on cartel activity in the area. Haystack had told Wes that sometimes when you can't find the source, let the source find you. The U.S. Government was known to pay pretty handsomely for actionable information on cartel activity.

Meanwhile, Marcia was getting comfortably accustomed to the RV resort where she and Wes had arranged a long-term lease. She was enjoying the warmer climate and just couldn't help herself as she texted a few provocative photos to some of her yoga buddies back in Minneapolis showing her lounging beside the pool. She liked this RV lifestyle and found a lot of common interests with a few of her fellow "campers". In fact she had even resumed her yoga discipline with a handful of trophy wives who, along with their husbands, had fled the northeast and upper midwest winter weather in the states and planned to work on their tans down south over the next few months. They offered yoga classes three mornings a week at the clubhouse and Marcia and pals had become regulars and usually enjoyed iced coffee poolside afterwards. Wes had become completely absorbed in his education of the border crisis under the tutelage of Haystack. While many women would have felt abandoned, Marica was an independent soul and put her free time to use getting to know the McAllen area, becoming acquainted with some influential people, asking a lot of questions, and listening even more. She quickly recognized that Texans, and particularly the McAllen ladies who she had come to know, were not shy on opinion. They had strong convictions on the government, immigration and drug & human trafficking and were only too happy to share those opinions.

Marcia had an epiphany one afternoon while having lunch

with two of her new friends at the Cultura Coffee House on 11th St. at the edge of town near Zinnia Park. The three of them had become particularly close, bonded by the common theme of domestic violence and sexual assault on so many young girls in the area. They had recently joined "Mujeres Unidas", a ladies auxiliary organization in support of the many innocent victims. At Marcia's suggestion, they had planned a "Walk in her Shoes" 5K crime awareness walk in a few weeks and were working out the details. As Marcia sipped on her Herbal Iced Tea and enjoyed her Chicken Caesar Salad, she could not help but notice a young girl in tattered clothing approaching along the railing separating the restaurant patio from the street. She reached out across the rail to slow her progress and asked her to join them for lunch. Marcia did not know this young girls' story, but she knew a hundred like her and she was instantly moved. As the young girl circled the railing and stepped onto the patio, a waiter quickly grabbed her by the hair and escorted her back to the street, chastising her as he dispatched her down the road. Marcia was repulsed, dropped a $20 on the table, excused herself to her friends, and caught the young Hispanic girl a moment later. "Habla Ingles"? inquired Marcia. "Yo hablo un poco" was the meek reply. Marcia mustered up her best Spanish, most only recently gained in her weeks in McAllen and said "Mi Español is muy mal pero yo tratare a comunicar contigo. Entiende?" Thankfully, the girl nodded her head. "Me llamo Elisa y tengo dieciséis años. Vivo en las calles porque no tengo una casa. Mis padres fueron asesinados y tengo hambre. Puedes ayudarme?". Marcias's heart dropped. She understood enough to know that the girl's name was Elisa, that she was sixteen, was homeless, and had lost both her parents to murder. Marcia was street savvy enough by now to see that this young girl was being prostituted, as evidenced by the tight fitting clothes, the push-up bra and the poor attempt at makeup. Marcia saw that Elisa was hungry and was desperate and could really use a hot shower and change of clothes. But she also suspected that some pimp was likely in the area insuring that he got his cut of the next "John" that wanted some action.

She held out her hand to Elisa as she nervously glanced around and they grabbed a cab back to the RV resort. She sent her into the shower with a change of clothes and whipped up a quick hot meal for her. She then helped her finish removing the garish makeup, swapped out a few pieces of clothing for a better fit, and was pleased at the transformation she had effected. She brushed through her ratted hair and gazed upon a pretty, young lady who appeared very tired and broken. She activated one of the sliders in the RV and escorted Elisa to the clean set of sheets. "Mil gracias por todo" said Elisa with eyes half closed and within minutes she was asleep. Marcia wiped the tears from her eyes as she pulled the sheets over her new roommate and begin to figure out a way to break the news to Wes.

"We have a what" said Wes as he tried to enter the RV with Marcia meeting him at the door that afternoon, blocking his path, and telling him to be quiet because they had a guest sleeping in the slider. She kept her finger to her lips and ushered him back out the door so that she could explain the day's events without waking the girl. Wes was not happy. "Do you realize that you have now placed her in even more danger since she will not be reporting back to her pimp tonight?. They'll track her down and kill her Marcia; these people don't mess around". "Over my dead body" Marcia spat back at him. "Well, that may just be the case and there's not much I can do about it. There are a million Elisas out there and you can't save them all. The government turns a blind eye this kind of stuff down here and is often even involved and taking kickbacks from traffickers. You are messing with something that is far bigger than both of us. Look, your heart is in the right place and God bless you for your humanity but you can't win this". "And what about you and Haystack?", she fired back. Are you not trying to do the same thing against the same forces?". "Well that's different", countered Wes, "we have a task force, informants, funding and hundreds of personnel while you are a Joan of Arc facing insurmountable odds and the prospect of getting "offed" at any time. You are messing with their cash, don't you see that?". "We'll see" was all that Marcia could muster and spun on her heel, entered the RV and opened a bottle of red wine while she got dinner started.

CHAPTER 47

THE CONFESSION

FATHER JAVIER MARADONA settled onto the padded seat in his confessional promptly at 7:30 a.m. on Saturday morning and began his daily devotionals just as he did every morning. Confessions were heard on Saturday morning, Thursday afternoon and by appointment. He did not anticipate much activity this morning but one never knew. Being a parish priest at a border town with a strong Hispanic Catholic population often presented unique challenges. Catholic priests were bound by their faith to never reveal to anyone the confessions of their parishioners, no matter how egregious. Further, a mesh screen separated Father Maradona's side of the booth from the other side so that he could see nothing more than a vague silhouette of the person asking for prayers of forgiveness. That secrecy was often enough to embolden sinners to pour out their souls. It was a very curious thing to the priest that drug runners, pedophiles and mules could operate without fear of retribution outside the church and yet beg for absolution once inside the confessional. It was a condition which tested Father Maradona's faith to the very limit.

Haystack lumbered through the heavy wooden front door of Holy Spirit Catholic Church, stopped in the sanctuary to bless himself with a splash of holy water, and then reverently proceeded to take a seat in a pew at the rear of the church. Moments later he lowered the kneeler, knelt down, bowed his head and began his personal conversation with his God; a God he was still trying to come to grips with. He had been raised a Catholic and fervently believed in God and in patriotism of the United States of America. But he felt those ideologies shifting despite his reluctance to let them go. He now had questions about the existence of a supreme being and whether or not his blind patriotism to the United States was in fact just delusional. The world was definitely changing. The wealthy and powerful were rising and leaving everyone else behind. Democracy was an interesting idea that burned brightly but short. With the widening divisions of our country today that flame was beginning to flicker. East, West, Muslim, Christian, Jew, Socialist, Capitalist, rich, poor, black, white; it seemed every issue could drive a wedge deep enough to cause violence on the other side. The polarity of opinion the last few years had sharpened societal norms such that restraint and respect no longer mattered. It was with these thoughts in mind that Haystack whispered to his God to forgive him his doubts and strengthen his resolve to remain a good Christian and serve the needs of the people he had taken an oath to protect. For at the end of the day, Haystack remained a man of principle.

Father Maradona was deeply in the middle of his devotions when he heard the confessional door open and felt the wooden structure shift in the presence of a large man whose outline began to take shape as he poured into the seat on the other side of the screen. "Thank you Father for all your blessings, my last confession was several months ago, forgive me, I am a sinner".

The priest gave the sign of the cross close to the screen and answered " Bless you my son, we are all sinners. Now tell me what it is that you seek?". Having heard the appropriate response, Haystack said "it's good to hear your voice Father. Progress is slow along the border and we seem to have hit a roadblock in our tracking of the Sinaloa Cartel mules. We are seeing unprecedented numbers of illegals making their way across the border but by the time we reach the scene, the mules are gone. We can't seem to make that connection to the next rung up the ladder. I was wondering if you may have any lead without, of course, revealing your sources?". There was a notable pause before Father Maradona answered. "My son, you know that I am as sickened by all of this cartel activity as you are and want to stop the abuse of these innocents. I am bound to silence, as you know, but I want to help and I can tell you that from this side of the confessional it is apparent that those who confide in me are merely the low level players. However that there is a discernible pattern in the confessions of several young Hispanic men who, when they choose, always confess their sins on Thursday afternoon. They all seem to come at about the same time, and from the lively chatter in the church while they wait for the others, they all seem eager to go from here to the Cantina Loco. They will know you so I would send someone else to see what they can find. I have nothing more". "Thank you Father, as always", said Haystack, "and I will see to it that the Agency makes a good donation to your church. Good day". "Go in peace with God my son", answered the priest as Haystack unseated his girth and gave the confessional one last shiver as he exited.

CHAPTER 48

LEISURE TIME

THE LEISURE TIME Grand RV Resort boasted unrivaled amenities in McAllen, Texas. RV owners had quarter acre lots with mature landscaping for a sense of privacy and each lot bordered the Executive Golf Course. Two tennis courts sat adjacent to a junior Olympic sized pool which offered cabanas and drink service. A third court was outfitted for pickleball. The clubhouse had a rec room and banquet hall and a cantina offered three meals a day, six days a week. It was little wonder that its 300 lots were in such high demand. Wes and Marcia had thoroughly enjoyed their time so far in McAllen, but the events of the past two weeks had taken some of the luster off of their stay. It was a tumultuous time for Marcia and she threw herself into weaning Elisa from the throes of her drug withdrawal. It was the most painful thing she had ever gone through. She had to watch Elisa endure the night sweats, the hallucinations, the nightmares and alternate periods of chills and fevers plagued her nights. But Marcia was resolute and her maternal instincts took over. After much holding and comforting the tide slowly began to turn. Elisa was becoming a normal and a very attractive young lady, and a bond formed between the two that would prove unshakeable. One evening Marcia trimmed Elisa's raven black hair, brushed it and braided it for her to give her a saucy, contemporary look. She went off to bed that night with a sense of contentment that she had never known.

When Elisa awoke the next morning, she was shocked to see post it notes on every item in the RV. Everything was labeled in English and Marcia saw in Elisa a very willing subject and a quick study as she went to each article mouthing the words. After only a couple of corrections, Marcia noted to Elisa that she had to make a grocery run and would be back soon. When she returned, she was delighted to see that Elisa had written a second word in Spanish under each English one denoting what the item was. And so the lessons began for both girls. They turned it into a game and giggled at their mistakes, but Marcia was seeing that she had a worthy adversary in Elisa and had to up her game to keep pace. Both Marcia and Wes still feared for Elisa's safety and therefore she was sequestered inside the RV for the time being, but they knew that would soon have to come to an end.

When Wes returned home that afternoon Marcia had his favorite Crown Royal Manhattan, served up, waiting for him in a chilled glass. He kicked off his boots, found his favorite chair and savored his drink while conversing with Elisa as Marcia cooked dinner. He had to admit that, despite his trepidation, he had grown fond of Elisa and the change had been remarkable. She had been transformed from a street urchin to a very appreciative young lady and she had shown a knack for the English language. Over a dinner of vegan chili and a fresh green salad, the three continued to work on their respective new languages.

Afterwards they went into the living room and played a game of Mexican Train Dominoes to help Elisa with her mathematics. Just before bedtime Elisa was allowed to watch a comedy show with her new family to assist with the language and to keep things light. She was usually the first to beg off however and went to bed early, allowing Wes and Marcia to develop a plan for the next stage of her transformation.

CHAPTER 49

CANTINA LOCO

WES HAD ASSURED Haystack that he would be extra cautious late that Thursday afternoon as he headed for the Cantina Loco to sniff around and get a feel for the place and the clientele it served. He was now on the payroll of the Customs and Border Patrol, under the supervision of Haystack, and was assigned as a Field Enforcement Officer in the fourth district which encompassed McAllen and the four counties along the border that abutted it. In the short time that he and Marcia had spent in McAllen, they both came to realize that this part of the country is where the real crisis lay and they were all in for committing themselves to exposing criminal enterprise here at the border. Wes was not yet a known figure about town but everything about him spoke "Gringo" which made todays task of making small talk with the locals that much tougher. He was not in CBP uniform but rather in denim jeans, plaid shirt, cowboy boots and the requisite cowboy hat to fend off the relentless sun.

The bar was much like any of a hundred others he had

frequented in his time, and he had been in many. He was very comfortable in a bar setting although from the looks of it this one would come with no frills. As he pulled his rented pick-up truck into the gravel parking lot, little whirlwinds of dust blew across the lot and coated everything for the umpteenth time. He made a mental note to not open a car wash in McAllen, as nobody seemed to wash their vehicles because they would look the same in a matter of hours. He pushed through the single screen door and noted that the temperature changed very little. An old A/C window unit rattled away on the far side of the room and a number of overhead fans lazily moved just enough air to keep the place tolerable. There was an almost even mix of Hispanic and Whites in the establishment and both languages could readily be heard. The juke box played a tinny rendition of some country western tune that Wes did not recognize. He glanced down the long wooden bar and settled onto one of the few open stools that remained. As he waited to be noticed by the bartender he casually surveyed the room. It was very busy for an early Thursday evening. Whites sat at tables with other Whites. Hispanics sat with other Hispanics, some even mixed congenially, and Wes quickly got the sense that this place was popular because the drinks were cheap and the botanos (appetizers) were equally inexpensive. Happy Hour was promoted from 4:00 to 7:00 each day and offered half price drinks and apps. For a man on a budget this was a pretty good night out for twenty bucks - if you didn't mind a little heat.

And if one needed another reason to frequent the Cantina Loco, it was Kristi. She appeared to be a mixture of White and Hispanic with the best qualities of each working strongly in her favor. She knew how to wriggle into a pair of tight jeans like skin on a bratwurst, and her loose raven curls and saucy disposition made her the desire of almost every red-blooded man in the joint. She was the unquestionable Madame of her bar, and she knew just how to treat the psyches of the untreatable. She effortlessly commanded total control of her room and it was nearly impossible not to surrender to her charms. In fact, Kristi Matheny was jokingly called "Crystal Meth" because she was so damned intoxicating. When she finally got around to Wes and tossed out her well rehearsed "what'll you have Hon"?, he was already enchanted. One glance into those almond eyes and that coquettish smile and he was sold. He knew that no matter what he had come here for, he was going to enjoy this evening. "Just a Corona draft for me darling" was his response; wincing as he said it and hoping that he hadn't been too quick on the draw. Kristi was unfazed, drew his draft into a cold glass and deftly placed it in front of him on a logoed coaster while pivoting and exhibiting that world class posterior as she sashayed down the bar to rescue the next thirsty soul.

CHAPTER 50

THE REVELATION

HAYSTACK ROLLED UP TO WES' RV site at 7:30 a.m. sharp in his F150 truck. He was just a little earlier than expected but he was anxious to get an early start to Zapata, about two hours west on Hwy. 83 where there was a reported major drug bust late last night. Wes had just finished showering from his morning run and was toweling off in the bathroom while Marcia dressed in the bedroom. Elisa was sitting quietly on the couch mesmerized by American cartoons when she heard the tap on the door. She froze. With no response, Haystack knocked again and then stuck his head halfway in and said "hello, anybody home?". He was shocked to see the pretty young lady sitting stiffly on the couch and said "well hello, who are you?". Elisa's fear was that this large man in uniform was here to take her away and tears began to roll down her cheeks. "My name is Elisa" was all she could muster in passable English and continued to tear up at the notion of losing this lifestyle she had so quickly come to love. Haystack quickly put her at ease and said "I'm not here to hurt you Hon". At that moment Wes entered the living room, buttoning up his shirt and quickly took stock of the situation. "Who is this pretty young lady", asked Haystack? "This is my daughter, Elisa", answered Wes, much to the surprise of Haystack. "I had no idea that you had a daughter, nor that she was here with you, but she sure is a beauty". "Thanks", answered Wes, "I'll meet you in the truck and tell you all about her. Let me just pop in and say goodbye to Marcia". As Haystack exited the RV, Wes hastily explained things to Marcia, kissed Elisa goodbye on the cheek and told her not to worry. "He's one of the good guys" he said on his way out the door.

The drive to Zapata was nearly two hours and provided plenty of time for Wes to explain the circumstances he arrived at and gave Haystack equal time to point out the hazards and the jeopardy he had placed his family in. For every explanation that Wes offered, Haystack had a counter position that always pointed to the dangers. Wes tried to close the discussion by saying that Marcia had completely embraced the challenge of stopping the human trafficking of young girls and would not be dissuaded from it. He concluded by saying how remarkable a transformation had taken place with Elisa and that Marcia was committed to helping as many others as she could. Haystack pulled the F150 off to the side of Hwy. 83, grabbed the steering wheel with both hands and, staring straight ahead, told Wes that he was fearful for Marcia's disappearance. He turned to look him straight in the eye and said "you need to give me your word that she will drop this and forget she ever met Elisa. We've come too far with things little buddy and I've enjoyed your company but you two are messing with the Mexican cartel and I can't tell you how many bodies there are buried across the desert of others for doing the same thing". Wes was silent for a moment but then answered that he did not think he could ever get Marcia to look the other way. "She's too strong-willed

Haystack and this event has changed her life". "Then you may want to think about pulling up stakes and moving along for your safety and that of the girls", finished Haystack.

The remainder of the ride was conducted in silence and soon Wes and Haystack rolled into Zapata County where the border town of Zapata served as the county seat. It was a fairly small, unassuming town of about 15,000 people of mixed heritage and its proximity to the Mexican border and its size kept it off the radar for most routine CBP checks. Therefore, it was the perfect place to smuggle illegals and drugs into the states. Fentanyl had become the drug of choice of late because it was easy to hide, created large profits, and had both clinical and recreational demand. First created in Europe in the early 1960s as an analgesic for surgery, it was introduced to the U.S. market several years later for relieving chronic pain. It was similar to morphine only 100 times stronger and therefore highly addictive. A tip last night from an informant in Laredo to a border patrol agent led to the interception of a cargo van crossing the desert into the outskirts of Zapata at about midnight. There was a large welcoming party awaiting them. The two male drivers were of Mexican descent and had no weapons, so they surrendered without a fight. The haul was nearly 140 lbs. of pure fentanyl with a street value of nearly $15 million. DEA, CBP and Homeland Security were all very interested in tracing back the suppliers and making an even bigger bust. Haystack was called in to conduct the interrogation as his territory included Zapata County.

CHAPTER 51

ZAPATA COUNTY

AS HAYSTACK and Wes rolled into the outskirts of Zapata they were struck by the starkness of the place. The relentless Texas dust covered everything and even as they drove down the barren streets, dust devils spun across the landscape before finally exhausting themselves under the forces of nature. The air was laden with the dust of the desert and the wind rose and fell rustling like sandpaper among the clutters of bunchgrass. A sandstorm could pop up in minutes and blot the sky from horizon to horizon. But for now, the sky was a pale blue like faded denim, the sun was hot, and the air smelled of dry timbers and an outhouse that stood too close to the sidewalk. Wes squinted into the distance, not caring how bright the sun was at the moment. He was anxious to see what lied ahead. Once they reached the squat, cinderblock county jailhouse, the odors changed to a smell of paint and recently sawn timber. It was apparent that someone had made a half-hearted effort recently to improve the looks of the building, but it was like putting lipstick on the proverbial pig. The effect was depressing but Haystack had seen it all before and strode into the building with authority while Wes followed with mouth agape. Sheriff Martinez knew Haystack well and greeted him warmly. He held local jurisdiction for criminal activity, but smuggling across international borders kicked this up to a higher authority and Haystack quickly took control of the situation. He and Wes were escorted back to the interrogation room where the two smugglers were shackled side by side to a large wooden table, resting uncomfortably on rickety wooden chairs.

Haystack looked the pair over in silence for a full minute as he assessed his opening remarks. The one on the left was a gangly young man with a sparse covering of hair on his lip which was his feeble claim to manhood. His eyes were flat and dull as charcoal and he would not look directly at Haystack, but rather stared nervously over his right shoulder. The one on the left glared directly at Haystack with merciless brown eyes. His features were hard and hIs moustache was dark and full, as was his head of hair - a head which rested atop a thick neck and a broad set of shoulders. Haystack knew who to direct his questioning to. "Habla Ingles?" he said, staring directly at the one on the left, but got no response. There was a protocol that Customs & Border Patrol personnel were required to follow when interrogating. But in this windowless, faded yellow room with no cameras, out on this barren landscape and with no witnesses, Haystack knew how to play his hand. He repeated himself and when once again he got no response he delivered his lecture in Spanish. "Let me tell you how this is going to go gentlemen. You have been apprehended with 140 lbs. of fentanyl which is enough to put you away for life. And while you may think you guys are real tough, you have no idea what can happen to some young, fresh meat like yourselves once it is served up to gang of hardened lifers in a crowded prison - guys who are in there for rape, murder, mutilation and unspeakable crimes of torture. Those boys know they will never get out of prison so there is nothing we can do to them to make their lives any worse than it already is. They play completely by their own rules and would like nothing more than to test their manhood on a couple of young bucks". At this point the one on the right put his head on the table and begin sobbing. "It doesn't have to be this way", continued Haystack, "but you boys have to give me something. To be honest, we don't really care about you but we want your suppliers. I can't for life of me figure out how the cartel risked that big a shipment of fentanyl in the hands of a couple of novices without weapons or backup. It doesn't fit the pattern, but I intend to find out one way or the other. You can make this easier on yourselves or you can make it harder. I don't give a damn either way. But if you work with me now and the information plays out, I promise to get you extradited to Mexico on a lesser charge and you'll be out of prison down there in 24 months". That information got their attention. The one ceased his sobbing and looked up while the others' cold eyes actually softened for a moment grasping for a ray of hope. "I'm going to give you five minutes to talk it over. You got one chance at this - that's it, so think it over real good and decide how you want to spend the rest of your lives". With that, Haystack got up and left the room.

CHAPTER 52

DOS AMIGAS

SPRING IN MCALLEN, Texas is almost nonexistent. The winter months are wet, short and cold and the summer months long, hot and oppressive. In between are wedged a few splendid weeks of weather that tend to fly by much too fast for the residents. It was on just such a splendid day that Marcia and Elisa were currently strolling the streets of downtown. Elisa's transformation from a ragged street urchin into a beautiful young lady had been remarkable under the guidance of Marcia. These two were quite a pair of head turners on the city streets and Marcia had fewer misgivings that anyone would ever know about Elisa's previous life. Nonetheless she dressed her in a large broad brimmed sun hat and a set of dark Ray Bans that only added to her allure. As she walked arm in arm with Marcia, her floral sundress with its spaghetti straps and its cinched waist accented her curvaceous body that had filled out so nicely under Marcia's care. Even her English had progressed so well that the casual observer would hardly pick up an accent. She was an incredibly gifted young lady and Marcia was eager to properly indoctrinate her into society. She was the adopted daughter of Marcia and Wes as far as anyone knew, and none had reason to question her origins. Today the girls were in and out of boutiques and antique shops, and each such venture was always a learning lesson for Elisa. Marcia would pick up an item they had not yet identified in their studies, pronounce it slowly and distinctly, and have Elisa do the same. Then she would explain its purpose and have her pronounce it again. Elisa's brain seemingly absorbed everything in her desire to please her new parents and fully embrace this lifestyle. The girls finished their day out and headed home to prepare dinner for Wes before he got there. Marcia had a serious subject to speak with him about and wanted to prime him beforehand with a cocktail and one of his favorite dishes.

The girls teamed up in the kitchen and Elisa had even begun to show an aptitude for the culinary arts. Tonight's dinner was pan seared sea bass with mushroom risotto and grilled asparagus with a lemon curd and garlic sauce. Wes was met at the door with his martini and the girls filled him in on their events of the day. Marcia allowed Elisa to do most of the talking to practice her new language, only interjecting to correct a rare mispronunciation. The two new "parents" sat back and soaked in the moment as Elisa excitedly recounted her day. They could not have been more proud if Elisa she had been their own child by birth, and it was one of the first moments that they felt like a true family. Once the day's update was done, they sat to eat their meal and Elisa and Marcia keep sneaking a peek at Wes to see how he was enjoying it. He couldn't hide his pleasure but his instincts were on high alert. "This is amazing", he said to Marcia who quickly deflected the praise. "I made the Caprese Salad, Elisa did the rest". "Well then I am all the more impressed and thank you both for this wonderful dinner. Now, let's take the easy out, put the dishes in the dishwasher and retire to the living room so that you two connivers can tell me what's up your sleeve. I have to believe there are strings attached to this wonderful evening".

Marcia was bemused by his statement but couldn't hide the fact that she had a hidden agenda. Shortly after they all settled in the living room she revealed her plan. "Honey, Elisa is adapting beautifully to her new life in McAllen and she now wanders freely without fear of recognition. But I understand your concern and those of Haystack's about her safety. And I share them. So tomorrow I would like to take her out and buy her a pistol and take her to a range for training." Wes was completely supportive of this idea because he was still haunted by the warnings of Haystack and in his short time with Customs & Border Enforcement he had seen the reach of the cartel. He suggested that they keep this off the radar for now. He agreed to buy the gun for Elisa and he would introduce the two of them to a young lady who could help familiarize them with gun control and gun safety without exposure to any outside influences that may tip their hand. Marcia was delighted at his willingness, Elisa was a willing accomplice, and it was decided that tomorrow evening they would go out to dinner and Wes would make the necessary introductions to facilitate this.

CHAPTER 53

HOME ON THE RANGE

MARCIA AND ELISA arrived first at the Cantina Loco and took a table for four on the outdoor patio. Wes had become a regular since his initial foray here several weeks earlier and had described to Marcia, in detail, Kristi and her impressive command of the place. It didn't take much acuity for Marcia to pick out Kristi and in fact she came to greet them at the table shortly after they sat down. "You must be Kristi", she said, and extended her hand in greeting. "I am Marcia, my boyfriend Wes is one of your biggest fans". "Well of course Sugar", beamed Kristi, he has become one of my favorites and has spoken so highly of you. So nice to meet you and who is this pretty young lady?". Marcia made the introduction to Elisa, who handled it flawlessly, and ordered a couple of club sodas with lime. "We are waiting on Wes and Haystack to join us at any moment", she said. "Perfect, I'll get your drinks and bring back some menus", and off she dashed to handle a few new patrons who had settled at the bar. Soon after, like a pair of Green Bay Packer linebackers, Haystack and Wes entered the front door and lumbered across the room to join the girls on the patio. After the requisite hugs and kisses all around, the fellas settled in and told about their day on the road and the challenges it brought. Kristi soon appeared with menus, two club sodas, and two chilled Dos Equis draft beers for the guys. "Are we that predictable?",

beamed Wes, to which Kristi responded "Hon, it's my job to know my customers". The evening was light and festive, and everyone was feeling good about the company they shared. Kristi was all over the table, explaining that one of her servers didn't show and she was short-handed so she was picking up the slack. "It's a common occurrence these days", she said, "no worries". And with that she disappeared again which gave Wes the chance to explain to Marcia and Elisa that Kristi was willing to take them under her wing and show them how to operate a hand gun. "She owns a little ranch just outside of town" said Wes, "and apparently she is pretty good with a gun, being a country girl, and saves empty beer cans for targets. She has agreed to give the two of you some target practice tomorrow morning before she opens her bar for the lunch traffic. The girls readily agreed and at the end of the evening when Kristi presented the check, arrangements were made for the following morning.

It was another beautiful late spring morning as Marcia and Elisa drove to Kristi's modest little ranch on the outskirts of McAllen. She welcomed them as they pulled through the gate and escorted them along a dirt path to where a clump of old tree stumps held empty beer cans. Before Kristi began the demonstration she asked the girls about their familiarity with guns. Marcia said she had been carrying a small pistol in her purse as protection since the death of her husband but had only fired it once. Elisa smiled and cracked that she had never held a gun but had been on the wrong end of several of them. The girls chuckled at that and Kristi pulled out her .380 Smith & Wesson and methodically took them through all the safety issues and do's and don'ts of firearms procedures. Once this was done, she struck her pose and pumped a couple of rounds in the nearest been can. One at a time, she showed the girls how to hold the gun, take the safety off, aim and gently squeeze the trigger. The noise and slight recoil were a little shocking at first, especially for Elisa. However, over the course of two hours they gained confidence and Kristi felt they would be able to defend themselves.

When the session was completed Kristi asked "who's hungry?" and both girls raised their hands. The three of them drove across town to a local BBQ hangout "The Joint" and grabbed a picnic table on the patio. Their waitress had apparently seen neither dentist nor hairdresser in the last decade and toted around at least an extra 50 pounds of girth. Nonetheless she was a spirited gal who recognized Kristi and asked her if she wanted "The House Especialidad". "Of course" was her response, and soon a delicious platter of pulled pork, beans, slaw, mac 'n cheese and Texas toast was delivered to the table, along with some sweetened iced tea with lemons. They ate way beyond their normal limitations but when the waitress offered Key Lime Pie for dessert they had to decline. The trio sat idly digesting their meal, enjoying their perfect afternoon and replaying the day's events. Suddenly Kristi stopped in mid conversation and dropped her head to avoid eye contact. Marcia immediately knew something was up and asked what the matter was. Kristi told her to casually turn around when she gave her the okay and to and look over her left shoulder at the man who was several tables away. She discreetly did so and noticed a man of Hispanic descent, in his mid-40s, with dark slicked back hair and the look of a cold killer. "Who is he"?, she inquired, but Kristi only offered "we'll talk later, are you guys ready to go?". They both looked at Elisa who had said nothing but sat there looking pale and they thought they noted tears flowing down her cheeks. They left their money on the table and left by the outdoor patio so as to avoid the table where the man sat.

CHAPTER 54

LUG NUT

"HIS NAME IS LUG NUT". The car fell silent for a moment and Marcia stared quizzically at Kristi and said "what"? as they drove away from the "The Joint". Kristi repeated "his name is Lug Nut but it's not his real name. It's his cartel handle. That guy at the BBQ joint, his real name is Raphael Santiago and he is supposedly deeply embedded in the cartel operations around McAllen. I'm told he owns a large car repair operation on the outskirts of town, thus the nickname, and it is suspected that he uses that and other nickel and dime operations around town to launder drug money for the Sinaloa cartel as well as to stash product on its way from Mexico into the states. I've heard some whispering around the bar from my Chicano locals that his car shop reconfigures vehicles to hide fentanyl and even abducted women across the border. He is well connected, you can be sure of that, and has many people in his pocket, even to include a local Circuit Court Judge, I'm told. He is a cartel kingpin in this area and is almost untouchable. He's been nabbed on suspicion of illegal activities several times before, but his lawyers have him out on the street the same day and there is never any evidence. He answers to a larger figure named Ezra. This Ezra guy reportedly controls much of the North and South American operations and even has some influence in the Asian and European markets. He is so well connected that he is deep into the pockets of the DEA and Border Control. Lug Nut is Ezra's "golden boy" for the lucrative southeast Texas border and he looks after him well. Marcia sat stunned as she took all this in and glanced in the back seat to see how Elisa was handling it. Elisa looked pale and kept her head down, shaken by the events which had just transpired. "Sweetie" she said and she reached back and grabbed her hand, "don't you worry, we will not let them get anywhere near you". Elisa shared a smile at Marcia which lacked any semblance of authenticity and Marcia knew that she was not the least bit convinced. She looked back at Kristi again with a growing sense of just how big an obstacle they were up against. "How do you know so much about these guys?", she asked. "Hon, I keep my eyes and ears open at the bar and I hear a lot of things that can sometimes slip out in the late night hours of alcohol conversation. I just keep my head down and pretend not to notice, and the Hispanics who frequent my bar don't know that I am bilingual. I prefer to keep it that way". The girls continued on their way home and Marcia got Elisa back to the safety of the RV, to comfort her, and to wait for Wes and Haystack to return from work.

Elisa slept fitfully that night and eventually made the decision to get out of bed and join Marcia for breakfast at daylight. When she stepped into the living room, still yawning and stretching out her tired muscles, she did not see nor hear Marcia stirring about, which was odd for this time of morning. As she rubbed the sleep from her eyes she noted a letter on the table which read..............Hey Sweet Stuff, had to go run some early errands. I'll be back this afternoon. Stay close to the RV and enjoy your day. Love You, Marcia. Elisa thought this strange, as this was the very first time that she had been left alone while Marcia was out and about. She was just a little put out but quickly fought that off as selfishness. She focused on her morning yoga ritual, some breathing exercises, and then made herself a health breakfast of yogurt, fresh fruit and granola. Afterwards she turned on the TV and watched a couple of her favorite rerun programs waiting anxiously for Marcia's return.

The drive across town to the auto repair shop was hot and dusty and became hellishly hotter as the sun rose higher in the hazy Texas sky. Marcia's route took her past the city and out towards the western outskirts where the buildings quickly fell into various states of disrepair and ramshackle huts served as homes for the many dirty, little children who swarmed the streets kicking worn out soccer balls with bare feet or riding decrepit bicycles across broken pavement. She grew uneasy as she drew looks from nearly everyone she passed. She was obviously a stranger to these parts and the people of these streets knew their own kind all too well. However Marcia was determined to get a better feel for this Lug Nut guy and what kind of operation he ran. It was much as she expected as she tentatively pulled near and saw open bay doors and several mechanic types lingering about in stained overalls; all sorely in need of a shave and shower, and passing around what she assumed to be a joint. Threadbare spare tires littered the dirt covered yard behind a chain link fence and cars of every size and description dotted the landscape. As she slowly drove past the place she could hear tinny Latin music playing from an old radio sitting in a front windowsill. She dared not stop, but drove on just past the building and parked in the shade of a nearby tree to get a better look. Within moments a rap on her window startled her and one of the mechanics mumbled out through smoke-stained teeth "Hola señora, quiere vender su carro?". "No, no" replied Marcia, "solo mirando para mi amiga. Yo pienso que estoy en el equivocado lugar pero gracias", and she quickly closed the gap at the top of the window and drove away cursing herself.

Boy, did I bomb that one, she said to herself, but at least she had the foresight to don a blonde wig, dark glasses and loose clothing before driving over so that any description would be pretty vague. As she drove back towards town her cell phone rang. It was Wes. "Hey, where the hell are you, I was worried". "Oh hi, I'm just out running errands and decided to let Elisa sleep in a bit this morning". "Well, you plan didn't work too well. She called me, concerned about your leaving her and I have to admit it was out of your normal routine." "To be honest Wes, I wanted to shop alone and get her something nice for her birthday. None of us know exactly when that is so I decided it was time for us to make one up." "Okay Hon, be careful out there and I'll see you when you get home. I'm headed there shortly. Elisa seems uneasy about being alone, which is a little out of character for her. Did something happen that I should know about?" "Oh, no, everything's fine and we'll talk about it all when I see you. Goodbye."

CHAPTER 55

EVERYBODY LOVES ICE CREAM

WES BOUNDED up the steps of the RV and through the door, delighted to see his two very favorite women were awaiting him. He received his peck on either cheek from the girls and settled into his easy chair as his favorite drink was offered. "How was your day?" queried Marcia. Wes took a deep breath to collect his thoughts. "Rough as usual," he responded, "and the Border Patrol and the DEA are getting more frustrated by the day. Team morale is low and these men and women are being overworked like a pack of Army mules. It seems that our government is oblivious about the onslaught of illegals and there is a serious lack of manpower to do anything about it. Other than that - everything is rosey. We did nab a few cartel guys with several kilos of fentanyl but we have to believe that it's just the tip of the iceberg. We think it may have been a diversionary "nab" to redirect our attention. There is something much bigger in the works, Haystack and I can feel it." He put down his empty drink glass with a ceremonial thud and announced that he was ready for another. "Hold on there big guy", chided Marcia, "it's only Tuesday - not the weekend.

You'll get some wine with dinner". Marcia moved to the kitchen to prepare dinner and Wes followed closely after, grabbing her from behind and nuzzling her neck as she stood over the stove. "What did you get her?", her whispered in her ear. Marcia shot him a puzzled look. "You know, for her birthday". "Oh that", she answered, "I just couldn't find the right gift", she said, putting her fingers to her lips. "We'll talk later" and they both glanced over at Elisa who was wrapped up in an old "I Love Lucy" episode.

Dinner, as usual, was superb and as the three of them sat contentedly in the living room digesting their meal, Wes jumped up and said "who's ready for ice cream?". He got no argument from the girls, and they all hopped in the car and headed into town. On the drive in Wes asked Elisa what she did all day to occupy herself while she was alone. She informed him that she was becoming more comfortable with the internet and was doing some exploring. "What did you research?" he asked, and was really curious as to what her interests were. "Places I would like to visit, career choices, things like that", responded Elisa. "The web can be a great tool", said Wes, "but it can be dangerous as well. Don't ever post your picture, name or location. There are predators out there and Marcia can help you navigate through it safely". When they arrived at the local Dairy Queen Marcia and Elisa ordered sugar free vanilla cones while Wes went all out for a good old fashioned banana split. As he wiped the whipped cream from his chin and attacked the hot fudge he smiled unashamedly and said "you guys are boring". "Maybe", said Marcia, "but at least we are thin". "Touché', maybe we should take a stroll around the lake and walk this off", said Wes. He got no argument, so they took off on a leisurely stroll around Lake Martin and returned to the RV just before dusk. It wasn't long before all were snugly tucked into their beds and fast asleep, with only the memories of an enjoyable day to tuck them in.

The blood curdling scream echoed throughout the RV at about 2:30 a.m. and jolted Wes and Marcia from their slumbers. Marcia was the first out of bed and the first to arrive at Elisa's bedside. She grabbed her by the shoulder and shook her into consciousness. "Honey, are you okay?". "I'm so sorry" sobbed Elisa, "it was that man from the BBQ place the other day. I know him from before. He does bad things to young girls". It took all of Marcia's strength to rein in Elisa's convulsions and she finally slipped into bed with her, hugging her and stroking her hair until she finally fell asleep. Coffee was brewing the next morning and Marcia rose to the enchanting aroma of it and slipped out of bed to join Wes in the kitchen for cup. Wes was curious as to what happened last night but Marcia only told him that Elisa was having nightmares of her past and decided not to offer any further information for the time being. When Elisa finally joined them in the kitchen later that morning, Wes inquired if she was okay. "I'm fine she said", noting the finger to the lips that Marcia was flashing her behind Wes' back. "You see", he said, "you should have had the banana split like me rather than that namby pamby fat free ice cream cone. Sometimes you just have to go all in and the say the devil may care". Elisa went over and gave a big hug to the only father figure that she ever knew and wished him a good day at work.

CHAPTER 56

FROM THE DEVIL'S CLUTCHES

SHORTLY AFTER WES left for work the next morning, Marcia and Elisa cleaned up the breakfast dishes and then Elisa grabbed Marcia by the hand and led her into the living room, asking her to sit. Over the next several hours she revealed to Marcia in agonising detail how she had been forced into prostitution as a young girl after her parents were murdered. She explained that she was one of a stable of girls under the control of the Sinaloa cartel in Mexico that was run by Lug Nut. She recounted how she and the others were often drugged and put into the streets to ply their trade. They all served at the pleasure of Lug Nut and his henchmen, and through that association she came to know Ezra through his infrequent visits for cartel business. Elisa suspected that because she was a little "fuller" than the rest of the girls, who were often malnourished, she was selected to be smuggled across the border and into the U.S. where she could bring more money into the cartel operation. She spoke freely about the well connected "Johns" that she was required to pleasure on behalf of the organization and how she was repulsed with each act and despised each filthy man.

She had determined that she would either find an escape or, short of that, to end her life. She finished by saying that said she was contemplating just such an act when her guardian angel, Marcia, pulled her off the street in McAllen on that liberating day that changed her entire life. Elisa's story was told with moments of heart wrenching sobs and Marcia cried right alongside her. In the end, she held Elisa's face between her hands, stared into those beautiful almond eyes, stroked that black licorice hair, and said "Wes and I want to legally adopt you as our own daughter". This brought a new wave of tears, albeit happy ones, and the two girls embraced long and lovingly. "Let's grab showers and clean up our act before "Dad" gets home", said Marcia, "and we'll celebrate your freedom from persecution and your new life as a member of our family." Elisa beamed with joy about the wonderful idea of having parents to care for her and who she, in turn, could care for.

Late that afternoon as Wes bounded up the steps and through the door, his instincts were quickly on high alert. There was nobody to greet him. Nobody to put a drink in his hand. Nobody in the living room watching the news, and certainly no aromas wafting out of the kitchen with the promise of a sumptuous meal. He froze in position just inside the door and called out "girls?", as his right hand automatically swept towards his holster. When he called out a second time he was relieved to see both girls come out of the bedroom looking all trussed up in nice clothing, faces made up, hair perfectly coiffed and both wearing precocious smiles. "Uh Oh", he smiled, "why do I get the feeling that this is going to cost me?". "Your genius never ceases to amaze me", chided Marcia, "and yes, it is going to cost you. We are going out for dinner tonight to celebrate". "And exactly what is it that we are celebrating", he asked. "We are celebrating parenthood', beamed Marcia. "I told Elisa today about our plans to adopt her and she is so excited."

Wes opened his brawny arms as wide as he could and welcomed both of his women into his grasp. "Hands down, one of the happiest days of my life, and to think I never even had to change a diaper". The girls chucked at this while Wes did his best to hide his tears. On the trip to the restaurant Marcia delicately explained to Wes about how their day was spent talking about Elisa's past, but careful to leave out the most sordid details. Elisa was quickly becoming "Americanized" and was in full headphone mode in the back seat so as not to have to relive that conversation again.

"The Weathervane" had become one of their favorite haunts in town when they had cause to celebrate, so their party was greeted warmly at the door and ushered to a booth in the corner. Wes eschewed the menu, when offered, pushing it aside and ordering a large Yuengling draft in a frosted mug. Marcia opted for a glass of the house red blend and Elisa had tea. When the waitress returned with the drinks, the girls ordered petite filets and Wes jumped all in for the 64 ounce Tomahawk Steak, despite the mild rebuke of his soul mate. "And gimme your biggest baked potato, loaded with butter, sour cream and grated cheese", said Wes, as he enjoyed rattling Marcia's chain even further. She merely rolled her eyes with a mock frown and the three of them spent the next hour enjoying one of the finest evenings any could ever remember. Dessert was out of the question; they had eaten all they could. However when the entire waitstaff approached the table signing Happy Birthday, Elisa had no choice but to blow out the candles, cut the cake and divvy up a piece for everyone. She looked at Marcia and Wes and her eyes said it all. She didn't need to speak. She was so grateful for all they had done and now they had brought her into their family. Marcia reached behind her into her purse and removed a small ring box with an opal inside which would now become her birthstone. A small diamond was mounted either side to represent her new parents. Then Marcia produced a second box, this one with a necklace and a matching opal pendant. Elisa looked lovingly at the gifts, then at her parents and was speechless as tears slowly found their way down her cheeks. "Welcome to our family" Wes and Marcia said in unison.

CHAPTER 57

RATTLESNAKE CANYON

IN THE EARLY first hours of the morning light, just as Wes was swallowing the last sips of his coffee, he heard the truck pull up outside. With a wry smile he glanced at his watch and noted that Haystack was as dependable as any alarm clock that mankind had ever created. A light beep on the horn confirmed that it was indeed Haystack and that he was eager to get this day going. Wes rinsed out his cup in the sink and planted a kiss of Marcia's forehead as she roused from the bedroom, pulling the ties of her bathrobe together. "Hey sleepyhead, we're off - wish us luck". And with that he was out the door. "Mornin' big fella" was the greeting he was met with as Wes jumped into the passenger seat of the F150. He sensed an extra shot of adrenaline from Haystack this morning and he knew just exactly why. After months of investigation and undercover work by the combined forces of DEA, Homeland Security and the Border Patrol, and in cooperation with the Mexican government, they had a breakthrough. Haystack's team had been given permission to cross the southern Texas border and conduct an insertion into an area of great interest to all parties called

Rattlesnake Canyon. It was considered the Holy Grail of drug and human trafficking activity for northern Mexico and today was the day his team had obtained authority to make a raid there. It had taken months in dealing with a lot of red tape but it had finally arrived. Haystack and his team had turned one of its smugglers from the recent Laredo bust into an informant and all of the information he provided seemed solid. The U.S. Air Force had supplied its latest generation military drone, the MQ20 Avenger Predator for this operation. It had been actively gathering information and mapping the canyon for the last several weeks, flying undetected from an altitude of 20,000 feet in preparation for this raid. Rattlesnake Canyon lay strategically just a couple of hours southwest of McAllen in an area heavily protected by the Sinaloa cartel. Haystack was as light-hearted as Wes could ever remember as they sped towards the Border Patrol compound on the outskirts of McAllen. They were on their way to link up with the rest of the task force. It was rare moments like this that made the grueling and thankless work of border enforcement worth it.

"Does the name Rattlesnake Canyon mean anything to you buddy?" queried Haystack as they drove the dusty desert roads just before sunrise. "Not really", answered Wes, "but it sounds pretty ominous". "And it should", said Haystack, "but not because of rattlesnakes, although I'm sure there are plenty of them there. But because the place has a real history that is intrinsically linked with the old wild west here in the U.S." "And I guess you are about to tell me something about that history - right?". Before Haystack could answer they entered the grounds of the outpost. He blinked his headlights twice on the tarmac then approached the four dark SUVs that were lined up. Haystack hopped out and shook hands with the squad leader, took a head count, and insured that all men were properly armed with tactical gear and wearing body armor and took a minute to briefly review the mission for the hundredth time. Moments later he and Wes jumped into the lead SUV, Haystack took the wheel, and the team was on its way in close formation with little regard for the speed limit. Haystack reached into the back seat and handed Wes a Kevlar vest and helmet and asked him to put them on before they crossed the border....."just in case, buddy". And with that, they raced west along Highway 81 towards Rio Grande City where they would cross the checkpoint into Mexico.

"There are countless stories written and passed down of the good old days in the wild west of the U.S., and many are often portrayed with a romantic twist" began Haystack as Wes sat back and listened. "But actually nothing could be further from the truth. As adventurous voyeurs pushed west across Texas, New Mexico and Arizona, looking to claim land and seek wealth, they faced extremely harsh conditions which growing up in the east could never have prepared them for. Many died, many turned back, and only the heartiest of them were able to transform into true Mountain Men and carve out an existence in the unsettled west. Legends were born, as men like "Liver eatin' Jones", "Naked Johanson", "The Preacher" and many others built their reputation by their toughness. "Naked Johanson" for example earned his name when an Apache war party surprised him while he was out on the prairie hunting elk. They stripped him naked and hung him upside down by his ankles from a mesquite tree and over a fire while they drank their firewater. These mountain men were a tough breed though and Johanson was able to elevate himself above the flames, untie himself and then run naked for miles to effect his escape. "The Preacher" likewise was caught by a band of injuns while trapping for pelts in the Lower Pecos Valley. He babbled (preached) non-stop for 6 straight hours until they thought he was crazy and ran him off without his horse, his rifle or his supplies. I'll spare you the sordid details about how Liver eatin' Jones made his name, but these were the first generation mountain men in the west. Their successors, or at least those who managed to survive, were fashioned of the same hearty stock as their ancestors, made names for themselves, and lived by their own laws. However, as the late 1900s turned a page into the next century, lawmakers slowly but inevitably tamed the West and these free spirits were pushed further and further south away from civilization. The U.S. was becoming too settled and too lawful for them, so they rode a few days south into Mexican territory and found an area called Rattlesnake Canyon. It was right in the heart of the Chihuahuan Desert - the largest in North America - covering more than 190,000 square miles. That desert however is ringed with mountain ranges such as the Sierra Madre, the Chisos and the Guadalupe. Those ranges created "sky islands" in the midst of the desert region and offered water and a cooler climate. This vast expanse of land was the perfect place for these real live cowboys to live as they chose. With time, many became settled there, rounded up wild horses, traded for some cattle, and built themselves some ranches. Many also took on Mexican women as wives and thus an entire generation of really tough half breeds was formed in the Chihuahuan desert region. They pretty much kept to themselves though as neither true Chicanos nor Gringos accepted them. Being spurned by everyone outside their community they formed "families" or cartels, the first to do so in Mexico and the first to capitalize on drug and human trafficking. Nobody outside the family was permitted into the business, and todays' thugs, people like Lug Nut and Ezra, are direct descendants of these earliest caballeros. They still hold a grudge and that's why they have a hard-on for us Gringos and why they are so ruthless". Wes shook his head in fascination of this great recanting of history but before he could ask any questions Haystack told him to put on his gear. The four SUVs pulled up to the Rio Grande City checkpoint.

Haystack flashed his badge from the lead vehicle, provided the approved code word, and the team barely slowed as it raced through the checkpoint, into Mexico, and down Highway 54 towards Cerralvo and Rattlesnake Canyon.

CHAPTER 58

THE DRIVE

ELISA ROLLED out of bed at the ridiculously luxurious hour of 8:oo a.m. As she sashayed into the kitchen to make her tea, Marcia looked up from her keyboard where she was ambitiously typing away. "Well, good morning Your Highness, shall I have the servants prepare breakfast and serve it to you in your royal chamber this morning?" she said with a wink. Without missing a beat, Elisa answered "okay, okay, you've made your point and I probably deserved that" she smiled back. "But you guys have really had me on the run these past few days and I guess all of the emotion and the excitement finally caught up to me". Marcia could not help but swell with pride at how well her young student had adapted to the English language. "Well, I'm glad you got the extra rest because we have another busy day ahead of us while "Dad" is out chasing bandidos. I've been researching on line how to generate a birth certificate for our newly adopted daughter. As it turns out, it's not as easy as I had hoped but we'll slog through the paperwork. And on that note, what middle and last name do you want me to put on these documents?" "I hadn't thought that far ahead, but what would

193

you say to me using Marcia for my middle name and your surname of Polk as my last name?". Marcia was humbled and quickly inserted the information into the on- line documents. While she typed, she had Elisa beside her to teach her how better to navigate the web. Every learning opportunity was eagerly grasped by Elisa and they were paying off.

"Let's take a trip to town today and scout out a few things" suggested Marcia. Elisa asked no questions, as she was always anxious to go into town. She popped back into the bedroom to slip into some white chinos and a light silk top with some comfortable deck shoes. Marcia approved when she came out and the two of them linked arms and headed for the car. The drive to town was lighthearted as the girls talked about trying out a new organic bistro on restaurant row just off of Alcazar Street. Elisa was surprised however when Marcia turned into a parking lot well short of their destination and asked Elisa to wait in the car for a moment.

She entered the front door of a large, unassuming brick building that read Bureau of Vital Statistics. She was back shortly with paperwork in hand explaining that this was the first step in making the adoption official. Lunch was next and Marcia lucked into a parking spot on Alcazar right in front of the Greenlife Organic Bistro. They were seated at a hi-boy table with a great view of the plaza and perused the menu. Marcia ordered a mint and matcha tea with coconut milk to drink and Elisa went for a mixed berry smoothie. For her meal Marcia had the arugula and beet salad topped with feta pine nuts and Elisa opted for a bed of crisp greens with carrots, tomatoes and blanched almonds, all topped with free range chicken and a champagne vinaigrette. "What a delight" said Elisa as she savored the last of her salad. "I breakfasted this morning as Your Highness and now I truly feel like royalty sitting here looking down on my loyal subjects while lunching on Ambrosia". The humor was not lost on Marcia and she just shook her head in admiration of how far this young lady had come. "Your Dad would starve here - no meat and potatoes. We'd better keep this place to ourselves". "Agreed" said Elisa and the two of them strolled out of the bistro as content as two good friends could be.

The trip home provided yet another surprise for Elisa as Marcia turned south off of Wieuca Blvd. and headed south into Hidalgo County. Elisa threw a puzzled look at Marcia but the only response she got was "it's a surprise". Several miles later they arrived at Moore Air Base, an inactive U.S. Air Force facility that offered a huge stretch of empty concrete and little more. Marcia exited the car and left it running, telling Elisa to get out as well. She dutifully did so and Marcia directed her to get into the driver's seat. She halted at the door...........me? drive? but I don't know how". "That is exactly why we are here my little one, now hop in and don't touch a thing until I get in the other side". Once they were buckled up Marcia slowly took Elisa through the different mechanisms of the car; brakes, accelerator, blinker and even the hands in the "2 & 10" position on the steering wheel as Marcia reflected back to her days in driver's ed so many years ago. "Now, slowly depress the accelerator until you feel the car move forward and get comfortable with a low speed. And remember, the brake is your friend so don't hesitate to use it". Elisa did as told and over the next hour under the patient tutelage of Marcia she gained confidence and was pronounced an excellent "first timer" when she finally surrendered the wheel back. On the trip home Marcia explained that Elisa needed to search the web for driving instruction courses and prepare for the test to get her own license. She readily agreed and was eager to open this new chapter in her life. Later that evening when Wes arrived home he had so many stories of his day that he was excited to share with his family. However, when Elisa greeted him as he entered and jumped into his arms with excitement he realized it was going to be about her tonight- not him. "I learned to drive today Dad", she beamed with all the simplicity of a child learning to ride a bike for the first time. He smiled and pretended to share in her excitement, with an arched eyebrow looked over to Marcia for an explanation. "We went out to Moore AFB today and practiced on the concrete runways". Wes readily acknowledged that there could not have been a safer place for a beginner to practice. However, he quickly put his serious "Dad" countenance on for a moment and cautioned that she must never drive alone until she had her license and her parents agreed that she was ready. "Of course Pop" said Elisa with a huge disarming grin, and at that very moment Wes realized he was no longer his own master.

CHAPTER 59

THE BODY SHOP

HIGH BEAMS AUTO Body Repair stood at the dead end of a dusty road on the southern outskirts of town. To get to it one must pass through the warehouse district, past numerous industrial plants, an auto graveyard and a lastly a run down used tire store before reaching the squat cinderblock building surrounded by a high, rusting chain link fence. The sign out front stated High Beams Auto Body in faded print on a rusty metal marquee. It was anything but welcoming, but Lug Nut didn't care. It was also impossible to get that far down the road without notice from some of the other proprieters along the route. Any unusual vehicle coming down the road was certain to prompt a call to the Auto Repair Shop and put them on alert. It's often been said that blood is thicker than water, and nowhere does that hold more true than throughout the Hispanic community brotherhood. So when Oscar, from the Bureau of Vital Statistics arrived at the garage in his dust covered Jeep Wrangler that morning, Lug Nut was waiting at the office door for him. Oscar exited the car and shook his head in admiration, not even trying to hold back his smile. "I'll say this for you, nobody gets near this place without you knowing about it. Every building I passed had somebody watching me. How many guys you got on the payroll anyway?" "That's none of your business, and besides, it has more to do with blood loyalty than the almighty peso", answered Lug Nut. "Yeah, right, whatever you say; see how long that lasts when the money dries up. Anyway, I may just have something for you in regard to that APB you put out some months ago about your missing girl". "Step inside and let's talk", answered Lug Nut. Oscar found an empty wooden swivel chair and sat down across from the desk where Lug Nut situated himself in an old leather chair that still managed to cling to a few remnants of the stuffing in the worn seat cushion. He ceremoniously propped his feet on the desk and said "now, whatcha got for me?". "A white lady came into the office yesterday and asked for the adoption paperwork for an orphaned Mexican girl. This is no young girl though, she's a teen and the lady was a little evasive about some of my questions. She was smart enough to not bring her in but I watched as she left and the girl who remained in the car outside had to be at least 16." "Okay good, describe the lady for me, did you get a license plate number?". "No, she was too quick, but she was a very attractive dame of about 40 with dark hair and one hot body brother". "Okay, keep me posted on any further paperwork she files. Ezra does not take kindly to having our merchandise disappear. We need to get our girl back and we need to send a very strong message to anyone who thinks about leaving our employ." Lug Nut slipped Oscar a "C Note" and thanked him for his information as he escorted him to the office door.

As Oscar pulled out of the parking lot a plain white cargo van with no markings passed him on its way in and drove immediately into an open bay in the building. The overhead door closed behind it and the engine was shut off. The driver exited and was met at the cargo door by two other Mexican nationals. The three of them carefully removed a burlap bag and unwrapped the twine. Inside was a young lady obviously heavily sedated. They placed her on a nearby mattress on the floor so that Lug Nut could examine her. He looked her over with care and pronounced her worthy for sale. "Give her another dose just to keep her quiet for a few hours and put her in that cavity in the Cadillac Escalade that we retrofitted this week. Tuco, you take her over to our contact out on Hermosa Drive and don't leave her until he comes up with every bit of the cash. And be sure and take your weapon". His thug did as he was told and rolled out onto the street carefully observing the speed limit. Lug Nut smiled smugly to himself as he returned to his office. Another good days' work and tomorrow would bring the prospect of yet another haul, this one a load of fentanyl coming in from Mexico that would reap a much bigger reward. His seedy empire continued to flourish in illegal activities and his only remorse was that he had yet to achieve a higher rung in the cartel's ladder. But he was ambitious, devious and ruthless and he was patient. Those traits would certainly carry him to greater heights, he was sure of it.

"Sweetie, I'm off to run an errand so why don't you use the time to study for your driving test?", said Marcia. She drove off and twenty minutes later was pullling up at High Beams Body Shop. Her arrival surprised nobody and in fact she had a small party of grease monkeys awaiting her. "I'm looking for the owner", she tried in English to see how far that would go. Almost in unison they answered "El dueno?" and pointed towards the office door. She moved confidently but cautiously through the door and confronted Lug Nut at his desk. "Hola Senor, habla Ingles"?, she managed as she eyed the clutter and grime. "Yes, I speak English. What can I do for you?", answered

Lug Nut while his beady eyes slowly took in every curve of Marcia's body. He was cautious. This middle aged white lady certainly didn't seem to pose any threat but it was very rare for someone like this to make it this far down the road without rethinking things and heading back out. "I recently had a flat tire and someone was kind enough to put on that pitiful small spare that the car manufacturers pass off as tires these days. I would like to have my flat repaired and put back on". Lug Nut considered the request for a moment and then answered "I'm busy until early next week and I only take cash". "Fine" she said, "how about Tuesday of next week around 11:00? Lug Nut nodded agreement and with that Marcia chose to exit by the side office door to the work bays, throwing the mechanics off stride a moment. She stopped momentarily to place her palm against the wall striking the pose of a fashion model. It was all they could to to contain themselves. "Por favor cuidado mi carro la proxima semana bien?" Thrown off by her ease with the Spanish language and even more so by how her mid-thigh skirt revealed a shapely pair of athletic legs, the men were mush. Marcia dropped her small purse and used the distraction to palm a micro camera in her hand on the wall and slip it into a metal groove in the dingy cinderblock while the men grappled to pick up the purse.. "Hasta pronto" she exclaimed as she threw her hand in the air at them and fired a coquettish smile on her way out the door.

CHAPTER 60

GIRL'S DAY OUT

MARCIA'S CELL phone rang late in the morning as she and Elisa were on the couch studying for the driver's license test. She was delighted to hear from Kristi, who was off until 4:00 p.m. that afternoon and was thinking about going to see Tom Cruise's "Top Gun" sequel, "Maverick". "Well of course we would love to join you for that", Elisa heard, "what hot blooded woman in her right mind could pass up the chance to see that hunk in action?". Arrangements were made to meet at the cinema at noon for the matinee performance. Marcia prepped Elisa on the drive over about the first movie so that she had just enough reference to understand the twists of this newest film. As expected, the girls were kept on the edges of their seats throughout the movie and as they left the theater each was anxiously sharing which part they enjoyed the most. In the parking lot Kristi glanced at her watch and said "I still have a couple of hours before I open up the bar. Would you guys like to do lunch?". "Of course", they both replied, and Marcia looked at Elisa and said "your pick Hon, you name it". "Anywhere but the BBQ Joint" she answered and they all locked eyes and had a good chuckle. "Okay", Elisa said, " let's celebrate my heritage and do the Taco Loco. Let's see what you gringos know about making tacos." Again, another chuckle and again a brief moment of pride for Marcia at how rapidly Elisa was developing a quick wit, a sense of humor, and the ability to convey it in English so well.

Neither Marcia nor Kristi was terribly excited about the taco place but they were happy to placate Elisa. The sign at the hostess stand read "please seat yourself", so the trio again found themselves at a hi-boy in the window watching the busy world of McAllen go by. Menus were soon brought over and a drink order was taken. When Elisa excused herself to go to the restroom, Marcia provided Kristi with a quick replay of the breakdown and the recovery period that Elisa endured just a few days prior. Kristi, now feeling like the big sister that Elisa never had, showed a flash of anger at the news and spat out "that man will burn in hell, Marcia and I would love to be the one to send him there". At that moment Elisa returned and the girls talked more about Cruise and the fact that a movie trailer shown prior to the film indicated he was currently making the next "Mission Impossible" film. "He is so handsome", mooned Elisa and they agreed on the spot that they would all go to see it together when it was released. "You know he is old enough to be your father don't you?", chided Marcia, "but I can sure can't blame you. Listen, once we get the adoption worked out we'll find you a good private school or Montessori for your proper education and you'll have a trove of boys to choose from. They will be fighting over you and then our only challenge will be getting that overly protective Dad of yours to let go." When the girls finished their meal they went arm in arm out to the parking lot. As they exchanged hugs and kisses, Elisa held Kristi a second or two longer than normal and told her how much she enjoyed her company. "Would you be my tia" (aunt), she asked. "I would love to baby girl and you sure know how to tug on one's heart strings!. "And did I tell you that I am learning to drive?", said Elisa. "Wait, what? Girl you sure are growing up fast. Slow down just a bit so I can enjoy the ride. And be careful out there will ya?" With that Kristi spirited her car out of the lot, kicking up a little loose gravel along the way. "Now THAT is how NOT to do it", scolded Marcia.

Upon the return to the RV Elisa continued her driver's license studies and Marcia quietly went to her bedroom to access the video of the camera she had placed at the body shop. It was motion activated so when there was nothing in the frame it was idle. When there were images they were fairly grainy and the audio was a little garbled as sounds of air compressors and wrenches torquing bolts competed with crude Spanish language from several grease monkeys. Every once in while she caught the image of Lug Nut moving across the screen, generally on his cell phone. But there was nothing to be gained as yet. She continued to stare at the screen without seeing as her mind raced forward. Just you wait you MoFo, you ain't as hot shit as you think, she said to herself. She couldn't wait for the day that this punk would be brought down for all of his debased atrocities. Her thoughts were brought back to the present when she heard Elisa call her from the other room. She wanted her to quiz her on the test. "Happy to do that Hon and I'm proud at how diligently you are studying for this." "Mom, can you explain diligent?". "It means with a great deal of effort", answered Marcia. She was challenging Elisa's great knack for absorption by continuing to use new words and thereby ever broadening her vocabulary.

CHAPTER 61

TURF WARS

IN THE NASTY little turf wars that inevitably happened between the supposed coordinated efforts of the DEA, Border Patrol, Homeland Security and the Mexican Government, there were often glitches. Finger pointing followed and damage control was often manipulated by using the press. Get too many players involved and eventually someone "on the take" would rat out the operation. That's how the game was played and Haystack had been in the game long enough to understand that. However on this mission he felt a little more optimistic that everything just might come together. Information of this operation had been limited to "need to know" only, and as he and Wes led the sortie south at breakneck speed, he continued to gain confidence that things may actually go off as planned. They raced along Highway 54 towards Cerralvo with nothing more to see than glimpses of creosote bush, mesquite, Mexican fire barrel cactus and yucca dotting the landscape among an endless sea of sand. The sky was a gunmetal gray and looked ominous as the threat of a storm approached. Haystack continued to check his monitor on the dash which gave him real time updates on the cartel complex outside of Cerralvo. The drone was performing beautifully with optimal images to his screen of the highest resolution known to technology. It communicated at rapid speed while also having the ability to jam any navigational, communication or reconnaissance drones that the cartel had in the air. That's why they dubbed the drone JAM and thanks to its state of the art features they were rolling in swiftly, their existence completely unknown to the cartel. Haystack and Wes watched in muted disbelief as the drone read the headline of a newspaper being read by an armed sentry on a bench outside of the complex they were headed for. Wes glanced over at Haystack and admired his calm demeanor, given that they were about to tackle a cartel stronghold. "Do you ever get scared about these kinds of things?" he asked. "I no longer have the luxury of fear" answered Haystack. "Fear is how you surrender your life - a little bit at a time. If we give in to fear then we take away from life. I refuse to live that way.". And with that, the discussion ended. Wes relaxed and thought about how far things had come and how far removed he now was from his days in law enforcement in Ohio. His career experience had vaulted him rapidly into a position of some prominence in the Border Patrol, and under the guidance of Haystack he had come a long way. He was sure that Haystack felt that way as well and he was hoping for an appointment of greater import in the near future. He was totally committed to this cause.

The embattled soul of the Sinaloa cartel operation in Cerralvo was Sergio Salamanca. He had been placed there three years earlier by Ezra and had done his best to run this critical distribution point for drugs and human trafficking according to cartel expectations. However time and talent have a way of taking the measure of every man. While Sergio was committed to the cause, he was after all only human. Three years without female companionship, without much interaction with the outside world, indeed, without even cable TV to divert his attention had left him questioning if this was his goal in life. It was only natural for him to let his guard down just a bit since the most excitement he had seen in three years was a cat fight between two female hostages. So when the four fully armed and staffed SUVs rolled into the complex his team was completely caught off guard. The firefight was brief but inevitable. Trained U.S. agents in full armor against unsuspecting and overmatched guards who quickly saw several of their buddies go down before deciding to surrender. Sergio was among the first to exit the compound headquarters with his hands up and the rest followed. A U.S. Military C130, which had been waiting for clearance from the raiding party, was on the ground within the half hour. The "undesirables" were rounded up and handcuffed, then put aboard the plane. Next came the hostages, eleven in all, who were unshackled and put aboard the plane after given a brief medical scan. The tubs of fentanyl followed; 22 of them in total with an estimated street value in the U.S. of more than $15 million. It was a banner day for the DEA and its mission partners. Haystack and Wes returned home late that day to a heroes welcome from their agency. The news of the success had hit the wire services before they even crossed back over the U.S. border.

CHAPTER 62

MEXICAN STANDOFF

"GANJA" tumbled out of bed and into a fog of consciousness at the first dings of his alarm clock. He trudged through the semidarkness of his small apartment and into his dirty bathroom, relieved himself, slipped into his greasy overalls which hung over the rusting shower rod and stared into the mirror. It was not a welcome sight, but one he had become accustomed to. Bloodshot eyes from too much weed and too much tequila the night before stared back at him. He ran his hands through his tousled oily hair and grudgingly accepted the results. By 6:30 a.m. he was out the back door and made his way down the alley to the High Beams Body Shop. As the lowest grunt in the pecking order, it was his duty to get the shop cleaned up and opened for business by 7:30 each morning. "Cleaned up" was a fairly relative term, especially when it comes to mechanics shops. However the shop had to be swept out each morning, the tools put back in order, and he had to to hose down and squeegee the grime from the floor into the grate located in the concrete floor of the middle bay. At least it wasn't Friday, he thought to himself as he wearily walked the six blocks to the shop. There was some consolation to that. On Friday his job was expanded to include to removing the grate and digging the accumulated sludge of the week from that grease pit. Then he would dump it in a barrel out back where it would be picked up sometime over the weekend. It was disgusting work but when you worked for the cartel your choices were rarely your own. Ganja unlocked the front door, flipped on the overhead lights in the bay, moved some equipment aside and began on the floor. As he worked his way along the wall, a small reflection of light caught the corner of his eye. He looked at the spot in the wall and saw what appeared to be a very small camera wedged into the iron framework which was bolted to the wall. His first reaction was shock. Was he being watched by his superiors? Was the entire crew under surveillance? He decided not to mess with it and left it untouched until he could ask the boss about it.

By 7:00 a.m. that morning both Marcia and Elisa were enjoying a cup of hot tea together and a croissant with some fresh fruit at the breakfast table. When they broke to clean up, Elisa volunteered to wash dishes and Marcia was happy to let her. She slipped back to her bedroom to scan her mobile and saw some early morning activity at the body shop. It looked harmless enough, probably just the cleaning crew getting the place ready for business. But she had seen just enough over the last few days to enforce her convictions that Lug Nut was running a dirty operation. Cash was exchanging hands, packages were packed into wheel wells, and something, possibly even a body, had been transported from one vehicle to another. She couldn't be sure, as her camera had a limited view, but she knew that something was rotten, and that Lug Nut was the scumbag behind it all.

Marcia had enrolled Elisa into a half day pre test driving course to insure her chances for passing. Class began at 10:00 a.m. and Marcia had her there early, chomping at the bit. She then took her time to leisurely make her way across town to the High Beams auto body shop. Her appointment was at 11:00 but she arrived a little early and found the place eerily quiet. No grease monkeys out front, no latin music blaring and nobody to greet her at the door, although she knew her presence was no surprise. As she entered the office she observed Lug Nut with his feet on the desk enjoying a cigarette as few people could ever enjoy a cigarette. He was pecking a few numbers into his cell phone but stopped when she entered. "Ah Señora, you are early. I will get one of the boys to bring your car in and change that tire out. Please have a seat." Marcia debated confronting this scoundrel about his activities but knew the odds were against her here on his turf. She decided to bide her time, hoping the camera had not been discovered and that it would produce more concrete evidence to take to the authorities. She took a seat in the cramped office and pretended to leaf through a tattered old Hot Rod magazine. Meanwhile Lug Nut disappeared into the bay and gave Ganja instructions to change out the tire. After a few minutes he returned to the office and acknowledged Marcia with just enough of a smile to be considered polite. He asked her if she would like a bottled water. Angered by all that he represented, and what he had done to Elisa, she could no longer contain herself. She was also just a little bit emboldened by the fact that she had her gun in her handbag which she clutched tightly to her stomach. "What I would like is to know why you continue to run this seedy operation and run drugs and humans through this shop. Have you no soul? Are you not human?" Lug Nut was thrown off, but only for a second. "So my hunch was correct and you were the one who planted a camera in my building?" Marcia did not hear the two goons who quickly swept into the office, wrestled her to the ground and muffled her screams with a chloroform soaked rag. While one stripped her of all her I.D. and smashed her cell phone, the other drove her car down the street and into the auto junkyard. A call from Lug Nut to his compadre insured that Marcia's vehicle was taken to the very rear of the lot and a crane immediately began to pile older junked cars on top of it. Within minutes it was as if neither car nor owner ever existed and all was quiet again in the barrio.

CHAPTER 63

CASTING NETS

ELISA SAT PATIENTLY on a bench out in front of the driving school where she had just delivered a nearly flawless execution of the driving test. Getting her license should be a breeze, she thought, but she had bigger concerns at the moment. She rechecked her watch and it was now 2:20 p.m.; well after the agreed upon hour for Marcia to pick her up. It was so uncharacteristic of Marcia to be late. In fact, if anything, she was always early. Elisa waited another ten minutes and then walked back inside the building to use a phone to call Wes. "What's up sweetie? What a nice surprise in the middle of the day". "Dad, I'm still at the driving school. Mom was supposed to pick me up a half hour ago. I've called her phone and I get no response. I'm starting to get worried - she is never late". "Okay, sit tight and I'll be there within twenty minutes. She is probably fine. Stay visible out front and don't go with anyone, do you understand?" Wes managed to keep his voice calm in order to not have Elisa panic, but there was no denying the gut punch that he felt in the pit of his stomach. On the drive to the license bureau he tried to call Marcia himself, to no avail, and tried to convince himself that it was just an oversight. Maybe she had a flat tire, or her cell phone was not charged or she had misplaced it somewhere. But his instincts from years in law enforcement, and more recently in border security told him that something was very wrong.

When Wes pulled up to the front of the licensing bureau Elisa rushed into his waiting arms. "Dad, I'm scared". "I know sweetie but we'll find Mom. Did she tell you where she was going?". "Only that she was running some errands and that she had to get a tire changed. The lump in Wes' throat prevented him from talking further at that moment. He put Elisa in the truck and made a beeline for Kristi's house, calling her along the way to alert her. They rolled into her drive spewing gravel as the tires ground to a quick stop. Kristi met them in the drive and Wes asked Elisa to go inside while they discussed a plan of action. Kristi approached Wes' window with a look of concern and said "this can't be good news". "It's not.....Marcia is missing, has been for a while now and we haven't been able to reach her. I just found out from Elisa that she was having a tire changed and I suspect she went to Lug Nut's place to confront him". "Dear God", cried Kristi, "surely not". "Look, if they've taken Marcia then they know about Elisa as well. Can you watch her for me while I sort this out?", said Wes. "You bet", she said, "they'll have to go through me and my AK47 before they get to her". With that assurance, Wes raced off to Haystack's and called from the truck to say he was on his way.

Haystack was waiting and hopped into the front passenger seat almost before Wes had stopped the truck and he asked for an update. "I'm afraid Marcia may have paid a visit to this Lug Nut character this morning to confront him and we haven't been able to reach her since". "Holy Mother of God, are you shitting me? We told her to steer clear. Jesus, let's get over there right away and see what we can find". They wasted no time in racing to the industrial section and had no regard for the "spooks" along the way who were sure to warn of their coming. They did a cursory pass of High Beam Auto Body and then circled back around and had another look at a very quiet yard as they slowly rolled by. Nothing caught their attention, no sign of Marcia's car, and they had no warrant so they had to play it by the book. A hundred yards later they slowly rolled up to the opening in the chain link fence surrounding the auto salvage yard. They noted the layer upon layer of rusting heaps of junked cars lined in rows. Being endowed with a lawman's curiosity, they decided to park and have a look. They were not here in any official capacity, just a couple of casual gearheads hoping to find a rare matching car part. The walked well wide of the office and seemed to engage in an animated conversation, pointing and laughing. But Manager Efrain Gavilianes had seen them from the moment they pulled up front and watched their every move from his little window that faced the junk-yard. He decided to give them a lot of leeway so as not to raise suspicion, but once they neared the back of the lot he decided he had better go out and run a little interference. The men had nearly reached the back and something on the back row caught Wes' attention. "Do you see that crumpled wreck of a car on the bottom, midway along that last row", Wes asked Haystack. "Yes", he answered, " and like you, I'm wondering why the paint job looks so new when everything around it looks like it has been rusting for years". Just then the attendant reached the men. "May I help you gentlemen with something?", he asked. Wes answered "I have a '66 GTO classic that I am restoring and I'm looking for a right rear quarter panel. Do you happen to have one on the lot?". "Please come with me", said Efraim and diverted them into the office where he accessed his computer. He checked his inventory and stated that he did not have anything that would fit that make and model. "I'm sorry", he said, "would you like me to do some research and see if I can find one?". Wes declined as he stared hard into the eyes of the Manager who likewise stood there unflinching. "Is there anything else I can help you with ?". Wes and Haystack realized they had likely overplayed their hand and could do nothing further without a warrant. They thanked Efrain and left the lot. Once they pulled away Efrain immediately placed a call to Lug Nut.

CHAPTER 64

WHAT NEXT?

"THIS ENTIRE THING SMELLS REAL FISHY", spat out Wes, as he and Haystack rolled out of the salvage yard. "That car we spotted is the same color as Marcia's and has not been there long". "Are you suggesting that it is her car and perhaps she's in it?", answered Haystack with a glance at Wes that showed his concern. "I pray that she isn't because there wouldn't be enough left to bury her. Can you get the authorities on the phone and arrange for a search warrant?" "I'm on it, he said, you just keep trying to reach Marcia - and remain positive buddy". The remainder of the drive was in desperate silence with Haystack arranging for a warrant and Wes trying in vain to reach Marcia. Each man was preoccupied with his own thoughts. As Wes rolled his vehicle up to Haystack's place the big man lumbered out of the truck and called back over his shoulder "I'll call you the minute I have a warrant. Chin up buddy, we'll find her". "Thanks" was the muted response but neither man was particularly convinced.

Wes raced across town to Kristi's place, knowing that Elisa

must be sick with worry by now about her Mom's disappearance. As he pulled in the driveway, Elisa rushed to the truck but stopped short, seeing nobody in the passenger seat. The fear was etched in her face; "where is she?". "I don't know honey but don't give up just yet". Kristi stood on the porch and, seeing the emotions of the two, did not need to be told how grim the situation was. As Wes held Elisa tightly he looked at the porch and shook his head from left to right. He put Elisa in the truck and met Kristi on the sidewalk, giving her a quick review of what had happened. She felt nauseous and turned her head to hide her emotions from Elisa. Father and daughter drove away in silence, wracked with worry about Marcia's disappearance. Elisa was the first to speak. "I just want to get home and find Mom there" she sobbed. Wes tried to do his part by saying "when we get home and see her and listen to her logical explanation, then we'll gang up on her". Elisa allowed a small chuckle but neither found much comfort.

As they headed towards home a police vehicle, with lights flashing and sirens blaring, raced by and Wes pulled off to the shoulder to accommodate it. As he returned to his lane, the lights of a fire engine appeared in his rear view mirror and again he pulled over. He resumed their journey with the hairs on the back of his neck standing at attention. Soon he rolled into the RV Park which was in complete pandemonium. It was impossible to not notice a huge cloud of gunmetal gray smoke billowing from the center of the resort. The pit of Wes' stomach did flip flops as he slowly worked his way past onlookers and approached his RV. He could get no closer than a couple of hundred yards and saw two firetrucks shooting water on the flames and the police cordoning off the site with tape for an official crime scene investigation. Elisa jumped from the truck and ran towards the RV screaming "My Mom, my Mom", but got no closer than the tape before several officers stopped her. Wes intervened and clasped Elisa tightly but was completely devoid of either thought or emotion. He could only stare at the collapsing structure of his home. An officer asked if he was the owner, to which he could only nod through his tears. "Do you know if anyone was home", was the next question. "I don't know, my spouse has been missing and now this". He was incapable of saying anything else as he and Elisa stood holding each other tightly and watching the scene in utter horror. "I will need you to come down to the station and make an official statement when you can". He nodded and agreed to do so as soon as he got his daughter somewhere safe. They stood there long enough to hear a firefighter confirm that there had been nobody in the RV. Elisa collapsed into Wes' arms and he carried her to the truck.

The trip back across town to Kristi's place was much more deliberate and with much heavier hearts. Kristi heard them pull up and dashed out, full of hope, but that was thwarted when she saw Elisa in a fetal position in the front seat with evidence of soot and ashes on her clothing. "Dear God in Heaven what has happened now?". Wes just nodded towards the front door and he and Kristi propped Elisa up and got her inside. Kristi took her back to one of the guest bedrooms and cleaned her up a little before she collapsed into the bed. Wes stopped at the living room and just unfolded into an easy chair, staring off into a void. When Kristi finally joined him, he told her what had happened. She sat with mouth agape and when he finally finished he asked if she could put them up for a few days. "Don't you even ask, you know my home is open to you as long as you need it. It's the cartel behind this isn't it"? "We don't know that yet but my guess is that you are correct". "I will find out who is behind this and I'll blow their asses off", she seethed as she leaped from her chair across from Wes. He calmly held up his hand and motioned her to sit. "You'll do nothing of the kind. Do you want to end up like Marcia? Or put Elisa in greater jeopardy? We are dealing with a powerful and ruthless criminal element and we are way outgunned. Let's be smart and us our federal resources to exact our revenge." Kristi calmed down, realizing the wisdom of his words, but said she would keep an ear to the ground at her bar, convinced that sooner or later some info would slip out from among her latino patrons and she would be all over it. Just then Wes' phone rang and he was asked to come downtown. As he made his way to the door he gave Kristi a big hug and made her promise that she would watch her back and watch after Elisa. "No funny stuff" he made her promise, and she reluctantly agreed.

CHAPTER 65

HELL HATH NO FURY

WES DIDN'T KNOW whether to spit nails or bawl. So much had happened in the last twenty four hours that his head was spinning and he was an emotional wreck. His girlfriend was missing, his home had been torched, and his daughter was a basket case as a result of it all. And yet he had to remain strong for her sake, even though he wasn't sure he could hold up his end of the bargain. He had a long career of dealing with these kinds of things in his former life but they were always somebody else's problem. Now they became his own personal problems and as he drove from the precinct back to Kristi's he tried to lay out a logical course of action. He pulled quietly into the driveway and was about to insert the key she had given him into the lock on the front door when it swung open. Kristi was waiting on him. "How is she?", was all he could think of at that moment. "She's asleep so we'll be quiet and let her rest". The two of them spent the next several hours in the living room contemplating what needed to happen now. Wes had to file a missing person report downtown in the morning. Then he had to meet with his insurance company and file a claim for the loss of the RV. He preferred not to drag Elisa through those unpleasantries and asked Kristi if she would be able to look after her and keep her shielded. "Don't fret, I'll keep her busy and safe and the three of us will get through this together - I promise. I've lost a husband, a brother and both parents so I know what grieving is all about. But you pick yourself up and you plod on because you have no choice. And that's what we'll do." Wes realized at that moment how important Kristi's strength was to him and Elisa and grabbed her hand, looking with soulful eyes into hers saying "I don't know where I would be without you". She squeezed his hand and answered "that's just what we do down here in Texas y'all", and forced a little smile that provided a momentary lift to the spirits.

Each went off to their bedroom but sleep escaped Wes most of the night. His mind was way too active and his anger was mounting. Revenge occupied his thoughts and would be the catalyst to get him through this. He marched through the police precinct door at precisely 9:00 a.m. and was directed to an office down the hall. The duty officer was on the phone so he respectfully waited outside the office when he felt a tap on his shoulder. He turned to see Haystack and was moved. "Thanks so much buddy, you don't know what this means to me". "Nonsense" was the reply, " you would do the same for me. And besides, I want in on a little bit of that kick ass revenge too. Do you think I'm going to let you have all the fun?". The levity helped, just a bit, and soon Wes filed his MP report with a description of Marcia and then he and Haystack exited the building. Reality had begun to sink in for Wes and he suspected that it was unlikely he would ever see Marcia again. "I'll drive", said Haystack, noting the obvious lack of sleep and the emotions that were playing across Wes' face. They hopped into the truck and Haystack flashed the warrant at Wes. "I already have men waiting for us at the salvage yard and in the field squeezing informants for information. Whatever happens from here - we'll deal with it.

As the truck turned into the salvage yard, the crane had already removed several heaps of deteriorating metal from the rubble above what looked to be Marcia's car. A forensic team was on standby and when the crane got to the white SUV on the bottom, it stepped in. Wes couldn't find it in himself to see what was inside so he turned and walked a few paces away. The Fire Department was on hand with its Jaws of Life and began peeling back the top of the car. Once inside it was confirmed that there was no body nor any evidence of blood-stains. Wes approached the vehicle with that happy news and spotted Marcia's purse. It was retrieved and verified that it held Marcia's I.D., and her cell phone. Relieved that he did not have to identify a body, Wes allowed for the purse and its contents to become evidence and as he walked back towards the truck he spotted Lug Nut being marched away in handcuffs across the lot. There is a God! Relief however was fleeting. Wes had been spared the horrific sight of a corpse, which meant that Marcia may still be alive. And yet, if she was alive and in the hands of this demonic group of thugs, there is no telling what she was having to deal with. At that moment his cell phone rang and an insurance adjustor was requesting that Wes meet him at the RV site. Haystack happily drove him over to the resort and the shock of chards of glass and burnt twisted metal left them in awe. They sifted through the ruins, but what remained was of absolutely no use. There was one exception. A fireproof safe containing all of his and Marcia's important documents had survived admirably. With Haystack's help, they lifted it into his truck bed. Wes completed his paperwork with the insurance inspector and the arson inspector assigned from the Fire Department, and he and Haystack were only too happy to leave the scene. Now, thought Wes, where the hell is Marcia?

CHAPTER 66

THE CANYON, CERRALVO

THE FACE he was now seeing in the mirror bore little resemblance to the smooth skin he'd seen twenty-five years earlier. Time and adventurous living, and the onslaught of the elements, have a way of taking their toll. His face was craggy but his mermeric opaline green eyes, edged with concern lines, still gleamed with intensity. HIs once dark hair now was tinged by gray along the temples. And yet he remained a striking figure, a limber man with the body of an acrobat standing at exactly six feet tall and carrying an efficient 185 pounds. In his early 40s, time had yet to diminish his physical skills and he projected pure power when those eyes bore into you. Ezra Castellanos Rojas stood at his marble bathroom sink, shaving his stubble and looking out over the vast canyon and the lands beyond. His fortress commanded the top of a hill overlooking the town of Cerralvo. It was formerly El Castillo de la Immacu-lada Concepcion, castle of the immaculate conception, origi-nally built in 1675 as one of a series of fortifications against invading tribes of Miskitos, whose ancestors came from Central America. With bastions still located on its four corners, it remained in amazingly good shape for its 350 years of merciless sun, withering winds and hurricanes - although it was fair to say that Ezra had invested heavily in its security and upgrading over the last several years. Now it was his prize and it represented the nexus of his empire. From atop the hill his influence was wielded across the country, the continent, and even, to some extent, in Europe. He gazed east, watching the sun rise and paint the sky in an assortment of pastel colors. He was at peace with himself at the moment, although still a little troubled by the American DEA bust of one of his drug warehouses on the outskirts of town recently. He had been busy planning his revenge through his underlings in the states.

The immense Chihuahuan Desert guards its secrets well, and nestled here among the splendor of the sky islands and the surrounding peaks, Ezra still felt pretty secure for the safety of his operations. Mexican bureaucrats kept a hands off policy as every politician, judge and police chief had been bought off. He was charitable to his little town of Cerralvo, a town of 8000, and made sure that the local community wanted for nothing. The citizens lived comfortably in gaily painted houses and enjoyed well maintained streets, running water and dependable electricity. They subsisted by farming the encircling hills or fishing from their panjas along the riverbanks or working at the sawmill. Those who didn't work there worked directly in support of the cartel operation in one way or another, such that no family in the town was untouched by its influence. Nothing happened that Mr. Ezra Castellanos Rojas did not know about. That also held true all across northern Mexico from Sinaloa on the west coast to Veracruz on the eastern border. This was his empire; he had worked hard to establish it and was now enjoying the fruits of his labors. In back of his elaborate fortress was a helipad where the latest McDonnell-Douglas Explorer Helicopter with twin Pratt & Whitney turboshaft engines stood ready to whisk him away at a moment's notice. Often that was a pleasure trip to his 150' Dynamiq SuperYacht moored just an hour's flight away in San Lucas on the southern tip of Baja. It was a one of a kind custom beauty designed in Monaco, engineered by a team from the Netherlands, and built in Tuscany. Its several staterooms allowed for many extravagant parties and its unique aluminum hull knifed through the water displacing 2000 horsepower provided by twin Rolls Royce diesel engines. For trips out of the country he had a Falcon 550 jet that was outfitted with plush sleeping quarters and a gourmet kitchen, and a fully stocked bar complete with Belique Crystal. Ezra's personal fleet of limos included a BMW 525 Sedan, a black Lincoln Town Car and a Navigator. Life is indeed good when you're on top.

As he finished shaving that morning and prepared to have his breakfast served to him, his satellite phone rang, identifying the caller as his lawyer, Hector D'Angelo, in McAllen, Tx. With a furrowed brow he pulled his robe together and sat at the breakfast table to sip his coffee and receive the news. He was aware of the recent events in McAllen; particularly as they concerned his "Capo" there, Lug Nut. In fact he has signed off on them with a cautionary word to leave no trace. "Digame", he spoke softly into the phone and then added "are you on a secure line?". "Of course Sir, I have my sat phone encrypted. We have an issue to deal with. Lug Nut has been taken into custody and booked for suspicion of abduction, possibly murder. They've thrown in arson on the grounds of having reasonable cause for that as well." There was a noted pause on the other end. "That fool, I told him to keep his emotions in check and not do anything stupid. Okay, pay a visit to him at the jail today and give the authorities your card. Tell them you represent him and want a list of charges and the grounds for those charges. I have a meeting in my Board Room within the hour. The heads of state for our country will all be present and I will bring them up to date. Report back to me when you find out what we're up against. Mr. Lug Nut may just have thrown a wrench into his future with the cartel and may have outlived his usefulness to us".

Once breakfast was finished, Ezra dressed quickly in a tailored suit from Georgio Armani and light colored sandals. He was the last to enter the Board Room and took his leisure in doing so. His Executive Board was already seated and was comprised of the Governors of each of the northern Mexican states contiguous to Chihuahua; Durango, Jalisco, Sinaloa, Veracruz, Nueva Leon, Coahula, and several others. Each sat rigidly at attention waiting for the meeting to begin. When Señor Rojas called for a meeting, you attended, no questions asked. Ezra entered the room behind dark sunglasses and with an unlit Monte Cristo Cuban cigar between his fingers. He slowly took his seat at the head of the massive mahogany table and methodically surveyed the room. His chin was templed by his fingers which bore gold rings encrusted with precious stones. Not a word was uttered until he finally addressed the assembly of men. "Who the hell are these Gringos that have the cajones to mess with our enterprise? I want them dealt with - comprende?" There was a consensus of nodding around the table and when Ezra spoke again he told of his conversation with his lawyer moments ago. "I want these guys to pay for their actions and I want Lug Nut out of jail.. I won't rest until this is done. I'll be talking to each of you individually as to how you can help make that happen". With that, he got up and left the table while the Governors dutifully broke into small groups to discuss how best to organize an effort to deal a blow to those brash Americans.

CHAPTER 67

THE SALON

ELISA ALLOWED herself a huge stretch and a yawn to match as she exited the bedroom. She shook her curls loose trying to regain her senses and then everything fell into place as she spotted Kristi making her way towards her. "Did you sleep okay Hon?". "Yes", was the muted reply, "I dreamed that Mom came home last night and were a happy family again". Kristi felt a pang of sorrow but recovered quickly. "Well let's hope that's one dream that comes true. In the mean time we need to get you some clothes since you lost everything in that fire. If Marcia does show up she'll have my butt for letting you look like a street urchin again. You get yourself together and I'll whip up a little breakfast. I have a big day planned for you". Elisa did her daily meditations and yoga stretches, just as if Marcia was beside her. An hour later the girls were on their way downtown to the McAllen Glamour Spa. It was an occasional rare treat for Kristi but a very first for Elisa. "How Do Hon?", they were greeted with as they brushed through the door. Carmen recognized Kristi immediately; "who is this cutie pie with you?" "This is my niece, Elisa, and a first timer, so sign us up for the works".

Nothing further needed to be said. For the next three hours it was pedicures, manicures and facials, and then came time for the haircut. When Elisa learned that, she pulled out her cell phone and showed a photo of Marcia. "I want a haircut like that", she politely requested. "Can do baby girl but that means about twelve inches off those beautiful locks of yours. Are you sure you want to do something that drastic?". "Yes I am" was her reply. "I want it to be a surprise to her when she comes home." "You got it Sweetie, let me have one more look at that photo". With that, Carmen went to work and within an hour created an ideal match of Marcia's cut. In fact she was so impressed with the result that she passed Elisa on to her make-up artist and asked Elisa to show her the photo as well. "Take care of this stunning young lady will you while I dial up Vogue Magazine. They do not want to miss this." Once completed, the transformation was remarkable and as Elisa and Kristi glanced at the image in the mirror both of their eyes began to water. "Hey you two, no crying okay....you'll mess up my make-up", warned Carmen.

The license bureau was barely a mile away and that was the next stop. Officer Matt Smentek ran a tight operation and also just happened to be a regular at Kristi's bar. She received a warm embrace when they entered and Kristi gave him a pleasant peck on the cheek. "Time to renew the license girl?". "Nope, this one's for my niece who will be getting her license for the first time. I imagine you heard about the fire at the RV resort?". "Yes I did", he replied. "Well that was Elisa's home and she's lost everything. So I thought our best first move would be to get her some official I.D." Matt expedited the request, under the severe circumstances and as a favor to the best bartender in town. Elisa ripped through the written exam and Matt personally took her out for the road test. Kristi waited for twenty minutes and when the two returned, a beaming Elisa told her all she needed to know.

On the way to the Barista Cyber Cafe, Elisa held her new photo I.D. up next to her Mom's photo on her phone. "I really do look like her don't I?", she asked. "Honey Bun, you could be her younger sister". The girls rolled into the cyber cafe, a Starbuck's knockoff, for a late coffee boost and a sandwich. It was busy with the right mix of Anglos and Hispanics. People chatted on cell phones and pecked away at keyboards. They had buds in their ears and listened to music or watched videos on their devices. Whatever happened to a cup of coffee and a newspaper, thought Kristi, while Elisa took it all in with the innocence of one seeing the scene play out for the first time. Kristi realized that this full diversion of activity was achieving its intended consequence. It was taking Elisa's mind off of Marcia, at least for a few hours. After a quick lunch and a short shopping spree to get Elisa enough clothes for a few days, the girls made their way home, completely exhausted, but on a high from the day's events. They were anxious to see Wes and learn if anything new had been learned about Marcia's whereabouts. "Your Dad will probably kill me when he sees how much hair we took off", moaned Kristi. "Or, he will be thrilled when he sees Marcia's younger sister", answered Elisa. "You are always one step ahead of me girl.", conceded Kristi.

Upon returning to Kristi's place, the girls learned via a phone message from Wes that there was no further information on Marcia's whereabouts. He indicated that he was fully immersed in the case and would not be home until late. A second message was from one of Kristi's employees who said he had tested positive for Covid and was in isolation. It was Friday afternoon and the biggest day of the week for Kristi. That presented a challenge. "Hey girl, how would you like a job?". Elisa was over the moon and loved the idea of this next phase in her life. "I need to call Dad first and make sure he is okay with it". "Of course, let's get him on the phone", said Kristi. Wes was not only okay with it but loved the idea of keeping Elisa occupied and in plenty of company.

CHAPTER 68

FEAR NO EVIL

RICARDO RODRIGUEZ, Jr. was the new District Attorney for Hidalgo County, which encompassed the city of McAllen. He had been overwhelmingly elected recently by a citizenship tired of gangs, cartels and criminals in general. He campaigned on "taking back the streets", and had been heavily supported thus far in his first few weeks in office. So as he was reviewing the cases of his two newest cell dwellers; Mr. Lug Nut of High Beams Auto and Mr. Efrain of McAllen Salvage Yard, he was disappointedly at an impasse. There was no presence of a body for the murder charge and there were no fingerprints of other evidence linking either of them to the missing person or the fire at her RV. Their lawyer sat smugly across the desk from him, knowing he had the upper hand at the moment and relished in it. "Unless you have any proof of guilt, I demand the immediate release of my clients" he said, as he stood and put his closed fists on the D.A.'s desk. In attendance was also the Circuit Court Judge who had set the bail at $50,000 each. He looked at Rodriguez and shrugged his shoulders in frustration. Bail was arranged and Hidalgo County jail's two newest prisoners walked free. A plain white panel van awaited them and they were quickly escorted away. They were being returned to their shops with explicit orders from Ezra, delivered by the attorney, to "keep your noses clean for now".

Haystack and Wes sat in a truck parked at the curb a hundred yards up the street. The took turns training the binoculars on the proceedings at the jail and then put a loose tail on the van as it made its way back across town. Wes was seething mad and digging his nails into the seat - it did not go unnoticed. "Easy buddy, I know you'd like to have a go at them but we have to stay hands off until we have something more". "Unacceptable" was Wes' firm reply, " and I'll tell you what we can do. Kristi runs a tight operation over there at the Broken Spoke Bar and knows every one of her patrons. That includes some 'marginal' characters of rival gangs who would love to see these guys taken down. With her acting on our behalf, I'll bet she can line up a few of her pals that we can pay to snatch Lug Nut off the street quietly. They deliver him to that DEA safe house out on Hermosa and we go have a chat with him." "Wow...you've given this some thought", answered Haystack. "But we can't have any loose ends or anything tying this back to us. Otherwise you and I will be ones warming the inside of a cell for kidnapping". "No worries.....Kristi would love to have a crack at revenge and you can trust her to keep quiet and make the arrangements. And you and I won't have anything to do with the abduction, we won't even meet the guys. We've got to bust some heads and I mean serious shit. I don't like the idea of waiting around, hoping some evidence will turn up, and then the worst this punk gets is a few years in prison with three squares a day, access to lawyers, newspapers, unlimited DVDs and watching football on TV while playing cards with his cellies. Haystack could only shake his head in admiration. Once he green-lighted it, he and Wes began planning the operation. There was layer upon layer of detail to be covered - weapons, logistics, contingencies and recruiting the personnel. The key was to get Lug Nut in transit once he left his house and before he got to "the hood".

Wes and Haystack drove the route between Lug Nut's house and the Body Shop multiple times. They watched his pattern, knew when he left home and how he arrived. The ideal spot for the abduction was at a stop sign about a mile from his house. He drove that stretch of road just after 7:00 a.m. each morning, usually with no traffic. Kristi had happily done her part and lined up a couple of thugs who she trusted. She passed along the information about where, when and how to make the grab and delivered a thousand in cash to each the night before. On the following morning the men were armed with 9mm Berettas in their waistbands. One stood at the corner holding a cardboard sign which read "hungry" and the other was crossing the street in front of Lug Nut's car just as it rolled up to the stop sign. Lug Nut's eyes were drawn briefly to the sign and in a fraction of a second, the walker was at the driver's door with his pistol pointed at Lug Nut's head while the other held the same position at the passenger's side. He leaped into the passenger seat, keeping his pistol in position and the other jumped into the back seat. "Drive" was the command from the back seat and Lug Nut did as told, feeling the cold pressure of a muzzle pressed up against the back of his neck. He pulled into an empty parking lot as told and was quickly blindfolded and had his hands bound with duct tape. He was pushed down into the seat and his two assailants drove to a prearranged spot behind a vacant building, left the car running, and walked away without looking back. Seconds later Wes came out of the shadows, put the car in gear and drove to the safe house.

Haystack was waiting with the garage door open and quickly closed it as Wes entered. The two men wrestled an unwilling Lug Nut out of the car and bent him over the trunk, patting him down. They found a .38 caliber and a cell phone which they immediately disabled. They spun him around and walked him into the nearest room where they secured him to a chair at a table. Wes removed the blindfold, stared into Lug Nut's eyes from across the table and asked "do you know who I am?" Lug Nut studied him for a moment and then replied "a dead man". "Wrong" he said before whipping his head forward. There was a crack of cartilage and a spray of blood as he shattered the man's beak of a nose. He slumped in his chair and Wes steadied him before whispering in his ear "I'm the Angel of Death and I'm taking you back to the hell that you belong in".

Wes and Haystack began filling a bucket of water and soaking a towel in it. "What are you doing?", asked Lug Nut, showing concern in his eyes for the first time. "I told you, I'm taking you back to hell". "What do you want from me?" scowled Lug Nut. Wes ignored the question and continued to fill the bucket. "Answer me" Lug Nut screamed. Wes looked at him with unflinching eyes and said "how long do you think you can hold your breath?". He had no reservations about torturing a scumbag like Lug Nut. While the politically correct crowd was against any form of torture in the States, Haystack felt differently, stayed mum, and sat back and enjoyed its merits. "If you wanted to kill me you would have done it by now" Lug Nut said with a slight tremor in his voice, feigning bravado. "That's right, I don't want to kill you. I want to watch you suffer and then I want to kill you", was the cold reply. With that Wes grabbed the back of his neck and plunged his head into the bucket of water and he placed the soaked towel over it. He held him there until the air left his lungs and was struggling for his life. Wes yanked the man's head out of the water and he drew huge gulps of air and started vomiting. He waited for the vomiting to stop and then plunged his head under water again. A few moments later he pulled him back up, allowed him to partially catch his breath and then he plunged him back down. He did it several more times and when he next pulled Lug Nut's head out of the water he did so with a demand. "I'll give you one chance at this scumbag. If you don't tell me what I want to know, my friend and I will happily watch you drown. Where is Marcia?". "I don't know" said Lug Nut, coughing and sputtering. Wes forced his head beneath the water again, Lug Nut was weak and didn't fight long. Wes knew he was on the verge of losing him. He pulled his head up and slapped him hard across the face. "Where is Marcia?". It was no use, Lug Nut lost consciousness.

CHAPTER 69

THE DASTARDLY DEPARTED

WES AND HAYSTACK left the room for a moment to confer on how far to push this next session. As a lawman and head of the DEA, Haystack did not want murder on his hands or to reflect upon his agency. Wes had less compassion on that topic but wanted to keep Lug Nut alive if only to gain information on Marcia. They made their points clear to each other and as they reentered the room they realized it was a moot point. Lug Nut was slumped in his chair, likely the victim of a heart attack at the punishment that had been meted out. "This is on me Haystack, you don't need to be any more involved than you already are. I'm the one who dished out the torture. I accept all responsibility and I'll handle things from here. "It's a little late for that buddy. I'm in up to my neck already but I think we've done the world a favor by getting rid of this punk. Let's clean up our mess." They loaded the body into Lug Nut's car and Wes drove it across town under cover of darkness to the Body Shop with Haystack following in the truck. Wes parked the car around the side of the building, wiped the steering wheel and door handles clean, and left the keys in the ignition, leaving

Lug Nut slumped behind the wheel. If the County Coroner did order an autopsy, it would appear that Lug Nut likely did in fact have a heart attack, as there was no sign of violence.

As Wes made his way home to Kristi's, he reflected on how much of his time and attention this incident had taken, and how he had been neglecting Elisa at this critical time. He was going to find a way to make it up to her. He arrived home just after the girls did and when he saw them step onto the porch he paused and looked faintly appalled with mouth hanging agape as he glanced at Elisa. His initial burst of joy turned to caution. Was that in fact Elisa standing on the porch or was it Marcia? Need and love were easily mistaken for each other and at this exact moment he wasn't sure which emotion captured him. He shook his head, quickly regained his senses, and admired the work that went into remaking his little girl in a shockingly close image of Marcia. Elisa sprang from the porch and wrapped Wes in an embrace that was unrelenting. She muffled her sobs in his arms while he inconspicuously wiped the tears from his eyes. When Elisa finally relinquished her hold, they walked hand in hand into the house where Wes got an enthusiastic recap of what they had been up to. She spent the next half hour telling him how Kristi had given her a position at the Broken Spoke Bar & Grill and how much she liked it. She pulled out over $100 in tip money that she had made on her very first night and told him that now she could save up to buy a car. "She's a natural Wes", said a very proud Kristi. "Being beautiful, bilingual and of course charming, she had my customers eating out of her hand. I'm not sure they'll ever settle for me again". They all had a chuckle over that and Wes was so pleased that Elisa seemed to forget Marcia, at least for the moment, and starting to live her life once again. Wes sat back and reveled in Elisa's excitement and allowed her to tell everything that she learned in the greatest detail as Kristi watched on as the proud aunt, occasionally exchanging knowing smiles with Wes at how good this diversion had been for Elisa. Soon it was time to call it a night and Elisa gave them both a hug and kiss and went off to bed. Wes and Kristi spoke in whispers for a short while, with him telling her that there was no further information on Marcia and that he had not been able to get anything out of Lug Nut. He stopped short of telling Kristi that Lug Nut died at his hands that night. He did not want her to be any more involved than she already was, and plausible deniability would be her friend if an investigation ever heated up. Wes did tell her that Lug Nut would be found in his car at the Body Shop tomorrow. "He likely had a heart attack as a result of tough questioning", said Wes, "and I wanted him to be with his 'Homies' when he is discovered". Kristi assured him that there would be no tears on her part and that this would be the last that they ever spoke of this subject. Wes had no doubt that she would live to that promise.

CHAPTER 70

THE TAIL

"HEART ATTACK MY ASS!". The words were literally spit out across the table by Ezra as word came in from his men in the field about Lug Nut's demise. "We know who is behind this and its those same two damned yokels and their cronies who pulled the raid on our warehouse a couple of weeks ago. I want information on these guys; I want names, positions, where they live, who they live with, where they eat and drink, and any vices they may have that we can exploit." His rant was directed at his closest held accomplices who sat quietly around the Board Table and made notes while he finished his fuming. There were six of them and they were as nasty looking a bunch of caballeros as you would ever want to mess with. That is all but Alejandro. Unlike his peers who were all large, heavily whiskered and scowling, he was a smallish man, about five foot five, slightly plump and unlikely to ever sport a speck of facial hair. When he shrugged at the sharp words being used, the skin at the back of his neck looked like a sharpei. His habit of staring at the floor while Ezra ranted only added to the image of his timidity. And yet he was the braintrust of the organization. He was the one who could crack computer codes, track electronic activity and hack into systems. Whereas his compadres ruled by fear, he ruled with his keyboard. Alejandro understood that it wasn't just knowledge that was power, but the application of knowledge that wielded power. He operated with impunity behind the scenes in a private office inside Ezra's fortress. And Ezra fully realized the value of his work. It was he who Ezra actually tasked with gathering info on the two primary hostiles and creating a complete file on each. The others he sent into the streets of McAllen to infiltrate the Hispanic communities and see what they could learn about the men's habits.

When your enemies succeed because they aren't constrained by rules, at some point you either have to accept defeat or tear up the rule book. It was a noble notion and one that Wes wanted to live by. He believed in the rule of law and that Americans should hold themselves to a higher standard than its enemies. The only problem was that it could also make the difference between winning and losing. And Wes was not willing to concede a loss to the cartel just to keep the moral high ground. It was time to be proactive and take the fight to the enemy's doorstep, rather than sitting back and reacting to whatever Ezra and company decided to dish out. Wes and Haystack had no doubt that there would be retribution for Lug Nuts' death and they wanted to press their advantage while they still held it; and before any more lives were taken. Haystack took the lead on this and rounded up his best men to plot a strategy to take down Ezra and deal a blow to his empire. While the southeast Texas Border Patrol's main office was in McAllen, it operated field offices, referred to as "resident agencies" in other cities along the border. Haystack assembled a team of the best and most seasoned field officers from each of those agencies and convened a meeting at his headquarters in McAllen. There were 14 in attendance that morning along with Wes as he commanded the head of the room and called attention to the image on the screen. "The man you see here is Mr. Ezra Castellanos Rojas. Mr. Rojas runs the Sinaloa cartel from his fortress in Cerralvo, Mexico. As you all know the cartel makes its money from a variety of criminal enterprises including arms trafficking, the drug trade, money laundering, prostitution, child pornography, smuggling and counterfeiting. In other words, if it is illegal they profit from it. Mr. Rojas has become a very rich man at the expense of Americans. It is time that we take him down. There was a noticeable buzz that ran around the room as the Border Patrol agents swapped looks and realized that they would finally get a crack at the top prize rather than dealing with the low level mules for a change. There was a lot of work to do and a lot of coordination with other agencies in both the U.S. and Mexico in order to green-light this bust, however this was an exciting first step and everyone in the room bought in with heart and soul.

After a long day, Haystack called an end to the proceedings and told everyone to go home and get some rest. Some of these men would actually be the "boots on the ground", while others would supply logistical support. First though Haystack had to establish an interagency network with between Border Patrol, Homeland Security, the DEA, the CIA, Interpol and the Mexican authorities. However, when it came to the last one he was very cautious because too many Mexican officials were so closely connected to cartel money. He did not want to tip his hand, so it was only on a "need to know" basis and for the purpose of providing cover for his team while in Mexico. As Wes and Haystack wearily trudged out of the headquarters that evening Wes said "I sure do miss my girls; why don't we head over to the Broken Spoke and take advantage of the all-you-can-eat Baby Back Ribs tonight?" "That's not on my paleo diet plan", smirked his nearly 300 lb. friend, "but you've managed to talk me into it you silver tongued devil. Let's take my truck and I'll drop you by to pick up your car on the way home". In route to the restaurant Haystack noticed a pair of headlights several vehicles behind him that had curiously taken every turn that he had taken. He even threw in a few extra turns and yet it remained cautiously back but nonetheless continued to follow their route. "I think we have company" he calmly said to Wes, who slowly dropped his visor and watched in the mirror. It was a black sedan with darkened windows. As they pulled into the restaurant parking lot, they lingered in the car a moment. The pursuing vehicle remained back about a hundred yards away from the streetlight and the headlights were shut off but nobody exited. "Yep, we've got a tail", said Haystack, "but I doubt they are stupid enough to create a scene at a crowded restaurant. Just keep your weapon handy in case". The restaurant was packed, the mood was light, and the two men were lucky to find seats at the bar where Kristi held court. "So good to see my two favorite men out tonight. Same as always fellas?" Both men nodded and when Kristi returned with their drinks Wes gave her a situation report. "Gotcha covered boys", she said, and selectively made the rounds to a few tables and had her guys on notice in case things got dicey. Fortunately for Elisa, Kristi and assigned her to work in the kitchen that night as an expediter so that she could gain an appreciation for the "back of the house operation. When Wes and Haystack had eaten their fill, Wes asked for permission to go say "hi" to Elisa in the kitchen. "Of course", said Kristi and he quickly went and gave her a peck on the cheek before joining Haystack for the ride home. The black sedan was still in place as they exited and it maintained surveillance from a distance. Rather than return

Wes to his car, Haystack drove to the downtown police station. It was only then that the tail disappeared. After waiting for a period of time, Haystack returned Wes to his car and cautioned him to "keep his head on a swivel and keep his weapon handy on the drive home."

CHAPTER 71

GREEN LIGHT

IT WAS uncharacteristic of Haystack to spend much time in his office. He was by nature a field operative and liked spending his time in the trenches rather than shuffling paperwork. So to see him at his desk the following morning with the door closed, operating the land line phone for hours surprised his staff. There were all kinds of speculation that something big must be brewing. He was methodically placing calls to all the requisite agencies who he would need cooperation from in order to execute a major cartel bust. It was no small feat to go after a cartel head and there was no end to the protocol. And yet, in the end, Haystack was thrilled at how quickly they all bought into the operation and pledged their full support. Nothing could spin the PR wheels of government like taking down the head of a Mexican cartel. It was risky, to be sure, but the reward was every lawman's and every politician's dream. Again layer upon layer of planning was required to ensure the success of the mission which was now being dubbed "Operation Pinball". Once the calls were completed and approvals were given to move forward, a teleconference call was set for 2:00 p.m. that afternoon.

Haystack sat rigidly at his monitor, took in a deep breath, and glanced one last time into the mirror, hoping to see a reflection that commanded authority. He was not disappointed as he flicked the strands of his red hair off his forehead. This was a big deal, even for a veteran like himself who had weathered many border battles. Taking out a cartel head put this onto a whole new stage. He took one last deep pull from his water bottle and then at exactly 2:00 p.m. he activated his screen. In each square on the screen, looking back at him was a tense looking member of the assigned task force. These were not the operatives who would be on the ground, but those who headed the various agencies and would be monitoring the operation from Langley. John Burke was the head of the task force, a 47 year old ex-Congressman and a tough, no nonsense fireplug with an I.Q. that was off the charts. He glared at Haystack with unflinching eyes. The Assistant Homeland Security Secretary was on the screen to his right. He was a retired police commissioner from Maryland and the most decorated cop in that state's history. Marc Raymond was Deputy Director of the FBI and a 20 year veteran of the agency. Admiral Day showed a deceptively calm manner. He was trim and sported youthful blue eyes despite his head of sparse gray hair. He would coordinate the military effort for the Joint Chiefs of Staff. To his left was Dr. Christine Russell, a 60 year old onetime bioterror advisor and aide-de-camp to Gerald Ford who wore a brown tent dress, had stringy matted hair and had to be really good at her job, or know secrets, to represent the CIA at this level. Air Force Major General Wayne Groves headed the Drug Enforcement Agency and was Haystack's boss in D.C.

Chairman John Burke took the lead from the outset, formally introduced Haystack to the task force members and asked him to provide an up to the minute sit rep (situation report) on the Sinaloa Cartel. Haystack had his three-minute recap committed to memory and recited it unflinchingly, concluding with his request to put an end to Ezra and foreseeably the cartel itself. "When you cut off the head of a snake, you take the snake out of play" he said. "Ezra rules with an iron fist and if we take him out there will be a vacuum in that cartel for a long time. Drugs, human trafficking, smuggling will all cease as a bloody power struggle will take place." Burke was the first to comment. "But you're a field agent for DEA, not a warrior. What makes you think you can head this operation?". Haystack didn't bat an eye, "nobody knows more about this cartel and its activities than I do. We facilitate drug busts and human trafficking at the border every week. The cartel operates in my territory and I have previously led a successful raid to Mr. Rojas' fortress. Despite it being heavily guarded, we rescued several hostages and took down a major drug haul." The task force members were aware of Haystack's success with his agency and nodded approvingly. Admiral Day was the next to speak. "We can get you all the military assistance that you require, but we would like to bring the troops back home as well. With a well guarded fortress, how do we account for the safety of our troops?". "I've thought a lot about that", answered Haystack, "and I think we hit Ezra where he's weakest. He has a yacht in San Lucas that he goes out on at least once a month. He has a proclivity for young girls and likes to take several along with him. Because of the nature of his entertainment, he wants minimal exposure on these trips so he sets out to sea with only a yacht crew of four (non military) and two or three muscle-heads. If we hit them hard and fast just before they shove off, the advantage is in our corner." More specifics were discussed over the next hour and eventually

"Operation Pinball" was green-lighted. One by one, Haystack addressed each of the screens representing the task force members, asked for what he would need from their agency, and then signed off. When his screen went dark you could have heard his sigh of relief from Las Cruces. He was overwhelmed with gratitude and anxious to start the planning.

CHAPTER 72

KEY WEST

A HURRICANE IS the most powerful force in nature. There is not even a close second. It can move thousands of miles, disrupt the lives of millions of people, and leave mass destruction and death in its wake. Dr. Karen Walk took one last cursory glance at her monitor; at the latest imagery collected by the geostationary satellites orbiting at 22,000 miles above the equator. A matronly woman with mostly silver gray hair pulled back in a tight bun, she was dressed in shorts that hit the knees and a matching sleeveless top to help fight off the heat and humidity that is synonymous with August in Florida. She reached to shut down her computer so that she could join her husband for dinner at the Lobster Trap, a trendy restaurant on Duval Street at the tip of Key West. It was their "date night" and he was excited about having his conch chowder and lobster mac and cheese - his two favorites. It was then that she picked up an almost indiscernible image on the screen over the Atlantic Ocean just off the coast of Africa. She halted and gazed at the screen again. The image now, compared with one taken hours earlier, was dramatically different. The mass of clouds had increased more rapidly than any storm she could remember in her twenty six years with the National Hurricane Center. She pulled her spectacles up by the chain looped around her neck, perched them on her nose and studied the screen more closely. "Much too fast" she thought to herself. "If it continues at this rate God only knows how massive a storm this could be." Most storms take many days to build, but this seemingly mushroomed in the span of just several hours. Karen picked up the phone and dialed her husband. "Date night is off", she said, and then explained why. He was disappointed, but his wife's mind was on anything but food at that moment and she intended to monitor this storm throughout the night.

When the tropical waters off the west coast of Africa are heated by a relentless summer sun, it causes vast amounts to evaporate into the atmosphere. That moisture rises into cooler air and condenses into massive clouds giving birth to a wide range of thunderstorms. Mix in whirling winds and the surface air pressure drops; the more it drops the more intense the winds. The sytem begins feeding on itself and creates an explosive centrifugal force that spins a solid wall of wind and rain. As Dr. Walk watched this one throughout the night, its fury multiplied and it began its murderous journey towards the Caribbean. As the winds increased to more than seventy miles per hour it earned a named storm status and was dubbed "Agatha", as the first named storm of the season. Dr. Walk put the Air Force on notice that a storm tracking plane should be readied if the storm maintained its current path. She then alerted all maritime agencies with her latest data and they in turn put all cargo ships and cruise ships in the Caribbean on notice to plan for alternate routes. The Coast Guard went into early evacuation mode procedures. NOAA began planning its first "spaghetti" models of the projected path of Agatha, and every meteorologist had it moving rapidly westward through the Caribbean and across the Gulf on essentially the same path. Hurricanes meander, they don't move in straight lines, and yet this one was doing just that.

This impending monumental storm was the backdrop for the actions of the strike force in D.C. that was busy planning Operation Pinball. If Hurricane Agatha did not dissuade Ezra from flying to his yacht, then the strike team would be there in San Lucas ahead of him. A Hercules C130 cargo plane, the longest serving and most reliable plane in the American military, had been assigned to fly a twelve-man Special Ops team to McAllen, Texas. They would pick up Haystack and Wes and fly across the Gulf to La Paz International Airport, about 2 hours north of San Lucas, so as to not draw attention. Blackened Sedans would be waiting on the team there to transport them to the Marina Puerto Los Cabos on the tip of the Baja Peninsula. This was a battle hardened group of warriors referred to as a Hatchet Team. Among their ranks were two weapons experts, two explosive experts, two medics, two radio comm men, two IT guys and two intelligence officers. They would lead the raid, with Haystack and Wes providing backup support and constant communication with the team in The Situation Room at the White House.

The President had privately been made aware of the mission, but it was "off the books" so that he could have plausible deniability as to its existence. Before the raid was actually executed however, he would make a personal call to the President of Mexico. He would have no problem getting his support. Cartels had no allies, least of all in Mexico where government officials often wielded less power than the cartels themselves. Meanwhile, hackers from the FBI had been able to access information from Ezra's computer and learned of his travel plans to

San Lucas. The flight plan called for his arrival in the Peninsula on Friday afternoon.

The first asset to be deployed was a drone. The United States Air Force launched its most advanced spy drone, the RQ Global Hawk, earlier that morning. This unmanned, high altitude, long endurance drone would monitor the skies over San Lucas and provide up to the minute surveillance, intelligence and reconnaissance (ISR) back to the Situation Room at the White House. The Task Force heads in D.C. would use that information to provide actionable information to the team on the ground, prior to its arrival and during the raid. The C130 was outfitted with complete tactical gear, to include H&K 417 Carbines for every member of the team. The aircraft and the strike team stood ready and just awaited the command to proceed.

CHAPTER 73

TRES AMIGAS

THE DAYS RACED by for Elisa and Kristi and it was therapeutic, as both were somewhat able to put the horror of Marica's disappearance behind them and move forward. They grew exceedingly close and Kristi recognized the gem she had in Elisa. She taught her every facet of the restaurant business and was in no way surprised at how quickly she absorbed it. She was a hit with the Broken Spoke clientele and even made two new friends among the staff who were a little closer to her age than Kristi was, and with whom she could share a little "girl talk". Haley was a little blonde dynamo who ran the front of the house and nothing escaped her attention. She had the panache' to smooth over any situation that arose and kept the staff in line. Jamie was the hostess who oozed charm and was that genuinely smiling person you hoped would greet you when you entered a restaurant and made you feel at home. She seated, greeted, assigned tables and ran the register. The restaurant and bar operation took on a new life, driven by this team of dedicated young ladies and became the "go to" place in town for drinks and dinner.

One day between the lunch and dinner shifts, Elisa joined Haley and Jamie for a trip to the mall where they enjoyed a late lunch and did a little shopping for cute, girlish outfits. Over lunch they became comfortable enough with each other to share some of their dark secrets. Neither of the other two could even begin to match Elisa's dark past however and when she took them down that road and bared her soul, they all had a hugging and crying fest. It was exactly the outlet that Elisa had needed for so long, and once she was unburdened, she would never again look back over her shoulder and relive the past. Later that night after Kristi and Elisa closed the bar, they joined Wes at home and had a lot of catching up to do. He had been consumed with some big plans in his own right and had been very busy. He could not tell the girls any specifics but indicated that he was on a big case. They in turn shared with him how well the restaurant was doing and how Elisa had made a couple of new friends that she went out with. Wes could not have been more pleased to see his daughter mature so quickly in front of his eyes and to embrace Kristi as a mother figure. "Dad, if Mom never comes back, do you think Kristi could be my new Mom?" The question caught him completely off guard and he and and Kristi exchanged an uncomfortable glance. "Sweetie, we are a family no matter what title you assign to Kristi, and nothing will change that. She loves you and I love you both and I feel completely whole when I have the two of you with me. God forbid, if Marcia never returns to us we have each other and I am grateful." That seemed to appease Elisa for the moment as Wes and Kristi exchanged subversive smiles without Elisa noticing.

It was late and the three of them took to their bedrooms to get a well deserved night's sleep. Around midnight Elisa was troubled with a nightmare about Marcia and tossed the bedsheets aside and headed for the bathroom. Passing her Dad's room, she noticed that his door was open. She continued towards the bathroom and then heard sounds coming from Aunt Kristi's room at the end of the hallway. The realization of what was happening was a shock. She had severely mixed emotions. Her two favorite people left in the world were in love and she should feel good. But she also felt betrayed because she was not yet ready to dismiss the idea that Marcia was gone. She returned to her room but sleep would not come. She wrestled with conflicting emotions until a strange aura made its presence into her room. It was Marcia telling her that everything was okay, that she was okay, and that she loved her and thought about her often. Elisa was not sure if she slept or if she dreamt, but soon the sun slipped over the horizon and she got up to join Wes and Kristi at the breakfast table. "How'd you sleep Swee Pea?", asked Kristi. "I had a terrible nightmare that kept me up most of the night", she answered. "Wanna share it with us?". "No, it was too weird and didn't make much sense. You know how confusing they can be at times.". Wes didn't like to hear that she was up most of the night and quickly changed the subject. "I got reimbursed for the damage to the RV and may begin to start looking for another." That statement seemed to shock Kristi and Elisa at the same time. "You know there is no rush Wes. I enjoy having you and Elisa as company and you are welcome to stay as long as you need to". Elisa looked at Wes for a reaction, but he was cool and noncommittal. "Then I should at least start paying you rent until we do find something else", was his reply. "I wouldn't accept it anyway, and I'm fine keeping the bright star of my restaurant close so that nothing happens to her". With that Wes headed for the door, chewing the last of his bagel and throwing a kiss to his two favorite women. "Love you both" he said and disappeared.

As Wes pulled out of the driveway he waved at the incoming car, recognizing Haley and Jamie as they pulled up to the porch. "We're heeeere" squealed Haley as she bounced out of the car and did a double somersault which landed her at the front steps. "Hey y'all, let's move. Tickets for the Beyonce' concert go on sale at 9:00 a.m." Elisa looked sheepishly at Kristi. "I forgot to tell you that Haley and Jamie invited me to the concert on Sunday." In mock indignation, Kristi stood with her arms crossed on the front porch and asked "and how am I going to run my restaurant with my three best employees out?". "Puhleese Aunt Kristi" all three said in unison. "It's a Sunday afternoon and we'll be there for the evening shift". "Okay", she relented, feeling a sense of satisfaction inside at how good the company of Haley and Jamie had been for Elisa. "But don't do a no-show on me or the next concert you attend will be the Mormon Tabernacle Choir performing "Amazing Grace" at your funeral!"

Wes drove over and picked up Haystack at his place for the drive downtown to his office. All the while they kept their eyes on the rearview mirrors. "Do you think we are being watched", asked Wes. "I would be surprised if we weren't", answered Haystack. "I'm assuming they are looking for a pattern in order to plan a hit. You know Ezra is not going to let this fly. We need to be on guard 24/7 until we execute this mission. In the mean time you might want to shack up at my place and throw the tail off of Kristi's place. Once the king is dead we can go about our normal lives again." Wes may just have found intimacy in his life once again but he realized this was the right thing to do in order to keep the girls safe.

CHAPTER 74

THE SITUATION in the Caribbean quickly moved from bad to worse. Agatha had strengthened to a Category 3 Hurricane overnight, buoyed by the warm waters of late summer and the absence of a weather system to stem its momentum. It seemed inevitable that this monster would continue to strengthen, as there was nothing in its path. It ripped across the island of Hispaniola, laying it flat, and continued its trek east across the Atlantic heading into the Gulf of Mexico. It was being monitored closely by all of the usual agencies, but none more closely than the strike team overseeing Operation Pinball. Ezra however maintained his plan to fly to San Lucas. It seems his depravity for young girls knew no bounds. So the C130 Hercules was loaded at Andrews Air Force Base and was ready to be dispatched with its team to McAllen, Texas. Four powerful engines roared to life. Inside, a dozen seats were bolted to the fuselage in back amid stores of food crates, med supplies and ammunition, along with the tactical gear that the team would require. Air Force Major David Pflieger took the controls, with the second seat occupied by Captain Travis

Beane who had been brought in for his experience in flying hurricane hunter aircraft during some of the most extreme storms that the Western Hemisphere had ever witnessed. It was a Cracker Jack team at the controls and they would need every ounce of their experience.

The C130 touched down at Moore Air Field in Hidalgo County, just outside of McAllen, with the deft precision of a feather falling on a pillow. It was a testament to the finesse of the flight team. Moore was a former Air Force Base which had been conceded as an agricultural airstrip. However, the Pentagon flexed its muscle and deemed this a priority one mission with arrangements to keep all civilian flights away for the day in the interest of maintaining a covert mission. Haystack and Wes met the aircraft as it taxied on the tarmac. The stairs were extended and they quickly climbed in and tossed their bags into the overhead webbing. They introduced themselves to the Hatchet Team members and then strapped themselves into a seat. The aircraft was not on the ground more than three minutes before retaking to the air. The flight time from McAllen, Texas to La Paz, Mexico was an estimated two hours and twenty three minutes. It would seem much, much longer.

Agatha was moving at a record pace east across the warm central Gulf waters and unleashed her fury as she quickly escalated to a category 4 storm. She was not following the rules of those storms that went before her. Contrary to moving in a zig zagging line like most, she was hurtling on a direct line across the sea as if she had a target in mind. Punching through the leading edge of the hurricane and scourged by whirling winds and blankets of hail and rain, the forty year old Hercules 130 took the beating in stride. Her wings flexed and fluttered and her four Allison forty six hundred horsepower engines chopped through the deluge at 300 knots. Dave Pflieger sat relaxed in the pilot seat, his eyes sweeping the instrument panel every minute. It was all he had to look at since the only view from the windshield was like looking at a washing machine in the soap cycle. His second, Travis, appeared equally calm and he too watched the gauges. They flew without complaint under incredibly appalling conditions while their crew in the back was tossed about like rag dolls. They stayed in radio communication with the rear cabin but had to yell over the noise of the storm to be heard. Eventually the aircraft soared into calm air and the sun glittered on its silver wings and the blue sea below. They had entered Agatha's eye and Pflieger banked and stayed within that eye for a few minutes while the crew gathered itself. Moments later they again entered the tortured gray wall and the aircraft shuddered as if under attack. Anything that wasn't strapped down was hurled against the bulkhead. Battered and lashed, Pflieger and Beane fought to keep the plane on a level flight path. The satanic gusts coming from flip-side directions nearly tore the plane out of the air. Never in their combined years of flying had these two veteran pilots encountered such incredible strength. "Let's take her down to twenty five hundred feet", said Pflieger, "and see if we can duck under these top winds". The move apparently helped and the storm finally seemed to spit the aircraft out of its whirling eddy like a projectile being dislodged from the throat of a choking victim. With each passing minute the conditions calmed a little as the aircraft began to outrun the storm. The men in the back noticed the difference as well and looked out the windows at the ground below. What caught their attention was that Interstate 5 running south out of San Diego was almost deserted. Unheard of at any time of day. And there was no signs of commercial air traffic, no aircraft in holding patterns, not even any contrails in the air. "Are we the only fools out in this weather" questioned one of the men.

Soon the C130 began its descent into LaPaz International Airport. It landed without fanfare on a private runway away from the main terminal. As the team gathered its gear and made its way to the exit, the pilots were standing at the door. "Sorry about that rough flight fellas", offered the Captain, shaking hands with each as they exited. "Was that a landing or were we shot down?", quipped Wes, and everyone had a good laugh, grateful to be on the ground. The black sedans were waiting on the team for the two hour trip to San Lucas.

CHAPTER 75

RETRIBUTION

ELISA'S PASSION for learning was exceptional. At the suggestion of her two new pals, Haley and Jamie, she began to study on-line to earn her GED. She dove into the program with the same intensity that she had applied to everything else. She not only wanted to learn, but she wanted to please her Dad and Kristi. She had planned on surprising them with the certificate but she couldn't contain herself. She shut down her computer when Kristi announced it was time to go to work. On the ride into town she sprung the surprise on Kristi who was of course so proud. They tried again to call Wes to share the news but with no success. She settled for a text message to him and Kristi asked when her Dad would be coming home. "I don't know Sweetie, he is on a special assignment and we have to give him some space". When they reached the employee parking area behind "Spokes Bar & Grill", Kristi noticed one of her regulars, Bruno, exiting from his car. He signaled to get her attention and the look on his face told Kristi that she should send Elisa ahead. "Hon, you go in and get set up for tonight and I'll be there in a minute". Bruno approached looking nervously in each direction and spoke quietly in Spanish. He told Kristi that High Beams Body Shop was open again under new management, and that Lug Nut's replacement had been hand-picked by Ezra from his ranks of thugs in Mexico. He heard from his sources that the drug and human smuggling would resume immediately and that cars were already being modified at the shop with false panels. Kristi was sickened by the thought of these young girls like Elisa being trafficked once again. Bruno added that the word in the street was the cartel was looking for Elisa. Ezra wanted to deliver a strong message to Wes that he was not to be toyed with. Kristi was enraged at this news and could barely contain herself. She slowly regained her composure because she had to. She grabbed Bruno's arm to steady herself and lead him into the bar to buy him a drink. "Me and my boys are here if you need us. In the meantime don't close this bar up alone at night, and keep that Glock handy.

The evening was non-stop and therefore passed quickly at the restaurant. All-you-can-eat Ribs has a way of bringing out the gluttonous worst in humanity, and Rib Night at "Spokes" was no exception. it was predominately pot bellied, testosterone loaded men that picked piles of ribs clean and washed it all down with pints of beer. It was not one of Kristi's favorite nights at the bar but the check average was high and the drinks rolled profusely, so the house did well and all the wait staff likewise did well with tips. Tomorrow would thankfully bring a return to sanity and to the return of the more refined Char Grilled Oysters and Chardonnay crowd. Kristi and Elisa locked up just before midnight and Bruno and a friend were sitting in their car. She waved a thanks to him and on the ride home Kristi mentioned to Elisa that she had to meet with a young couple in the morning who were getting married and wanted to have a catered event at the restaurant. "No problem", answered Elisa, "I can keep myself occupied for a couple of hours working on my GED. You do what you have to do and don't worry about me". Kristi flashed her a grateful smile but in the back of her mind she was concerned about what Bruno had told her earlier and wanted to insulate Elisa. She didn't want to alarm her by sharing Bruno's information, but she didn't want any undue exposure either. "Okay, but stay here at the house and don't go anywhere. Be careful of anyone who comes to the door". "Yesssss Mother", Elisa derisively said while she rolled her eyes skyward.

The next morning Kristi was up early, showered, and headed out the door, planting a kiss of Elisa's forehead and saying "I'll be back in a few hours". It was the perfect opportunity for Elisa to go on-line and work on her GED. She was completely engrossed with her nose in the computer screen when she heard the doorbell ring. She eased back the curtains and saw a man standing on the doorstep who she did not recognize. She knew not to answer, so she called Kristi. "It's okay Honey, I've been expecting him and he has something for you". Elisa answered the door and the man offered a set of keys, pointing to a car in the driveway and saying "Your Mom and Dad asked me to deliver this to you". She covered her mouth to muffle the scream, but the emotions went unchecked. "OMG"! The tears rolled down her cheeks and before she knew it, she hugged the man on the doorstep. He accepted the embrace, somewhat uncomfortably, and then jumped into a car nearby with another driver and the two of them disappeared. Elisa immediately called Kristi, still sobbing, and Kristi responded, "you don't think I was going to haul your ass to college every day did you?". She called her Dad next but was unable to reach him. The next call was to her new pals, Haley and Jamie. She reached Haley first. "You got a what? A Mustang? And I'm driving around in this beat up old Corolla with 180,000 miles on it and worn out tires." They had a chuckle and Jamie offered her congrats as well when she was reached.

After her meeting with the young couple that was to be married, Kristi deviated from her route home and headed to High Beam Auto Body. On her way, she called Elisa to check on her and to tell her she would be there within the hour. She arrived at the garage around noon and, as is typical with the Hispanic culture, things had slowed by midday and two of the mechanics were slouched in their chairs, nodding, while the third navigated a porn site that he attempted to hide as Kristi entered. He looked up as she breezed through the door with a sense of purpose. "Puedo ayudarla señorita". "Si, yo necesito neumaticos nuevos para mi carro" "Donde esta su carro?", he answered and Kristi led him out back to where she had parked her car. They walked all the way back to the far end of the lot with Kristi pointing out her car. As they approached, she pulled her 9mm Glock from her purse and with two muffled spits, she dispatched of the vermin. She returned to the office where the two other lay napping and emptied the remains of her magazine into the two of them. "Vaya con Dios MoFos" she said, and then searching to make sure there was no video cameras around, she drove away with a clear conscience that Elisa would be safe and that no young girls would ever be trafficked through this hellhole again. As she crossed the river from Hidalgo County into Brooke County, she lowered the window and dropped her Glock into the river.

CHAPTER 76

"BURN THE SHIPS"

THE PREDATOR DRONE was performing its job flawlessly. At 10,000 feet up it was too high to be detected from the ground and it was clear of any air traffic lanes. Even at that height the drone could read a license plate on the ground and was in fact transmitting that information to the team back home in the Situation Room. License tags of Ezra's party were being recorded and traced. The heat signatures from where the yacht was moored showed eleven yellowish glowing figures on the large monitor back in D.C. That matched with the latest intel reports that there were four armed security men, four from the yacht's crew, and Ezra and his two young hostages. Alpha team had the lead vehicle and raced due south on Highway 1 with four heavily armed special agents, while the other three vehicles followed closely in its wake. Driving conditions were miserable, as Hurricane Agatha continued its westward trek and caught the convoy in transit. Rain pelted the windshields mercilessly and black billowing clouds in the distance showed no sign of it ceasing.

Haystack and Wes sat in the back seat of the fourth vehicle relaying updates from the Command Center to the others. They had just been told to slow down and get there safely. The yacht would not be leaving the harbor in this weather. Wes began to have a little sense of foreboding with all that they had faced. He looked over at Haystack who was beginning to strap on his tactical gear. "We sure picked a fine time to go on a Mexican vacation. No hammock among swaying palm trees on the beach and no Margaritas. We've got to fly through a Category Four Hurricane, and then run into it again on the drive to take out a drug kingpin while keeping our men and those two young hostages safe. Do you ever think that it's all for naught? We take out Ezra and then the other Mexican cartels fight a bloody turf war for the territory in which hundreds will likely die." In his usual cool manner, Haystack just smiled and continued to strap on his gear. "How is your knowledge of history old Buddy?" "If you're talking about Mexican history it's pretty weak but I'm guessing that's about to change." "Yep, It was right on this very stretch of the Peninsula where we are now that in 1519 Hernando Cortez landed with 600 men and 6 ships. He was sent to conquer the Aztec Indian Empire for Spain. The journey was tougher than any could have imagined though and by the time they finally reached land his men lost their appetite for fighting and wanted to return to their home country. Cortez sent the message through the ranks that there was no turning back, but his men were angry and rebellious. That night with his most trusted aide, Cortez burned the ships - now there was no going back. Within a couple of years his men defeated the Aztecs and claimed the land for Spain". "So", said Wes, "the message is that we're committed to this raid and there is no going back." "That's right buddy, burn the ships."

The convoy slowed and eased into parking lot as far away from Ezra's yacht as possible. The intensity of the storm shielded its approach and nobody was foolhardy enough to be out in this weather. The four teams did a systems check and got final word from the Situation Room that there were two figures looming outside of the yacht at mid-ship, presumably guards. Beta team had the weapon experts and its team departed the vehicle first to clear the route. They halted within 100 meters of the yacht and identified two armed men bracing against the sheets of rain and oblivious to their presence. They took up their positions and gave the "all clear" for the rest to follow. Once its two snipers had the men zeroed in on their sights they requested permission to engage. The okay was relayed down from D.C. With two quick muffled tap taps from each sniper, the guards slumped to the deck. The team held its position to see if anyone inside had been alerted, but after a minute all remained quiet. One by one they quietly slipped up the gangway and gathered either side of the large double glass sliding doors and the Beta team leader gently pulled to see if it was locked. It was not. Delta team was to remain outside on watch while the other three breached the cabin. With the flick of his hand, the team leader slid back the door and the room exploded in activity and yelling. They swept in with rifles drawn ordering everybody down. The two remaining guards quickly realized they were over matched and fell to the ground. They were put on their stomachs, searched, I.D. was taken and then they had hands and legs cuffed. The rest of the team worked its way through the ship finding the Captain, First Mate, Chef and Chief Steward. They were all escorted back to the lobby to join the others. Ezra stormed out of his suite which was all the way forward and vented his rage as he came. "You have no authority to invade my ship. Who are you people? He was dropped to the floor and cuffed as well, struggling and screaming obscenities in both Spanish and English. He was ignored while the two young girls were located and brought out with the rest. Once all were accounted for Ezra was wrestled back to his cabin and cuffed to a chair by his hands and feet. He was left there alone while everyone else remained in the lobby.

Haystack entered the room, an ominous presence under any circumstances, but now toting a rifle, sporting body armor, and drenched from the rain, he didn't look happy. He addressed the room. "We are with the United States Government and your boss is being arrested on multiple international criminal charges. We can take you in as accomplices or maybe we can just assume that you only work for him and don't know anything about his activities." He glanced around the room seeing looks of desperation give way to a measure of hope and some eager nodding. "That's what I thought. You two", he said, pointing to the guards, "you leave immediately and forget you ever knew this man or we'll be back looking for you to join him in prison". They were uncuffed and couldn't get out the door fast enough. "Captain, I'll need you and the Chef to stay a while. You other two, you are responsible to see to it that these two young ladies get back to their parents. Don't disappoint me - now go. Forget you were ever here". They were all four released from their cuffs and seen to the door. "Chef, my men here have had a long day and would use a great meal. "I'm assuming you can make that happen?". "Yes Sir, I can" "Good, okay men, make yourself comfortable and we'll have a good meal at Mr. Ezra's expense. Alpha Team, contact the Situation Room and give them a "sit rep". Tell them we will be extracting some vital information from our host for the next several hours. The two other team members on Haystack and Wes' squad were interrogation specialists. They would be given the time needed to extract information but first Haystack asked for a few moments with Ezra to handle a personal score.

Wes and Haystack entered the master suite and shut the

door behind them. Ezra was strapped to the chair, squirming, and opened his mouth to scream at them but Wes was too quick. He delivered a slap across the face that sent blood and spittle flying. "You made the mistake of taking something that belonged to me", he growled, staring into those black eyes shrouded in evil. "Go to hell" was his answer. It was the wrong one. Wes hit him again, harder this time. "Let's try again, where is my wife?". "You will never see you wife again and you and all your filthy men will pay for this with your lives". "I had hoped you were smarter than this. You'll see me again soon enough". He and Haystack left the room and joined the others awaiting the Chef's creation. The two interrogation specialists were next, entering Ezra's room and closing the door behind them. But not before asking the Captain to turn on the sound system and provide some music to muffle any screams. The men all passed the hour enjoying the decadent luxury of a $250 million yacht and Wes went to the wine cellar to choose some good companion bottles for dinner when he learned what the Chef was making. Once dinner was ready, the two interrogators joined the others and they all enjoyed a fantastic meal. The interrogators went through their notes and recounted names, addresses, weapons & drug caches and smuggling routes that they had been able to extract from Ezra. It was a treasure trove that would at least dismantle the cartel. They began transmitting the data back to D.C. as soon as they finished.

The men helped the Chef clean up while Wes and Haystack joined the Captain in the control room. They asked if he would take the men out on a little cruise around the tip of the Peninsula and just off the western shore of the Baja where the waters were known for its great whites. The storm had passed and the blue waters of the Pacific awaited them. He was happy to accommodate and promptly started the engines while the men gathered outside on the deck to enjoy the sights. Wes and Haystack went and retrieved Ezra and wrestled him to the aft deck. They unhooked the lifeboat from the winch and hooked him up in its place. Ezra fought and screamed violently, demanding to know what was going on. They stripped his shoes and socks from his feet and removed his pants. "We decided to treat our men to a meat piñata" said Wes. Ezra was writhing and screaming out of control while they chummed the water below and then soaked his bare legs in the chum. He fought with every last ounce of strength he could muster until he was drained. Finally he was reduced to sobbing and begging for forgiveness as he was lowered over the side so that his feet just touched the water. The ocean was already frothing as the sharks were drawn in by the chum and it was only seconds before the first bone crushing bite was heard and Ezra unleashed a cry that sounded like it came from another world. The next crunch followed seconds later as an even larger shark attacked the other leg and soon a flurry of them were working their way up the torso and fighting for the remains of the bloody stump.

CHAPTER 77

WHO'S THAT LADY?

THE TAKEDOWN of Ezra Castellanos Rojas and his empire was monumental and sent scores of sensational headlines searing across the internet. Information was scarce however because this was a "Black Ops" mission not acknowledged by the U.S., while true responsibility lay buried deep within the bureaucracy of Washington, D.C. The President denied any knowledge but did offer a remark saying that any time a drug cartel was dismantled it was a win for all people. The Mexican President offered similar remarks and likewise claimed not to know who was behind it. Nonetheless, it was a huge sting and the fact that it was conducted off the radar made the rumors run rampant. It had a domino effect that continued for weeks as thugs across North and South America, and even on the Asian continent, continued to get rolled up in the haul as federal agencies infiltrated and dismantled the network piece by piece.

Back in McAllen, Wes and Haystack were happy to be on home turf once again and content to stay out of the limelight. Kristi wrapped Wes up in a big bear hug upon his return and said she was so happy that she had not been aware of what he was up to. "I would not have slept a wink" she said. "Well, rest easy now because thousands of trafficked people and tons of drugs will be removed from the clutches of these butchers. Imagine if your loved one had disappeared and you never knew where they were taken or if you would see them again. I would love to see the face of every parent who is reunited with a missing child. That would be all the reward I could ever want." "Yes, said Kristi, "and that one hits close to home for us. I am so proud for what you have done". "I have you to thank for supporting me through this and keeping Elisa safe all the while. If I had lost her I don't know that I could ever forgive myself." They settled comfortably into the couch, Wes reached up and doused the lights and they buried themselves under the blankets for the evening spending the next several hours making up for lost time.

The passing weeks brought a return to normalcy. Wes, Kristi and Elisa grew ever closer and even Haystack found himself a "little old gal" who snatched his heart away before he knew it. The Big Bear was really just a soft touch after all as it turned out and much of their leisure time was spent together around the Broken Spoke. The restaurant was enjoying huge success thanks to the talents that all the young ladies brought to bear. As the dinner shift was winding down one night, Haley and Jamie told Elisa that they would be headed to the U of T for fall semester classes. She was excited for them but would miss them terribly. But she too had been advancing her career at the local community college and was studying Hospitality Administration. She was even ambitiously writing a business plan for an outdoor expansion to the restaurant. Kristi felt it was time to have a private party at the restaurant to celebrate all the good fortune they had shared and to send off Haley and

Jamie in style. They had it on a Sunday night when the restaurant was closed. The evening proved to be fabulous; the Chef knocked it out of the park, the wines were splendid, and they even got Haystack and his new "filly" to dance. As the evening closed and Kristi locked the doors, they decided to have a nightcap. While the three of them sat in the afterglow of a perfect day she said she had an announcement. Wes and Elisa were taken back but sat silently. "I am with child" she said. Those words hung on the air for several seconds before anyone could react. Elisa screamed and ran up to hug Kristi while Wes did he best to hide his blubbering and made a mess of it. The three of them hugged and danced around giddily. Wes had a moment to reflect back on all that he had been through and realized he finally had a chance to slip back into normal life and make it all work. With all of the burdens gone he could make his life whole once again and he reveled in that moment. It took a while for the three of them to regain their composure, but when they did, the ride home was all about "baby", until Kristi finally called a halt and said "Hey, let's take this slow". They continued their drive home and as they turned into the drive and parked, they got out of the car and held hands as they made their way to the front of the ranch house. It was at that moment that they noted a car parked out in front of the porch and the movement of a rocking chair on that porch froze them in their tracks. Silhouetted by the light from the overhead lamp was a figure calmly rocking there and looking at them. They were all incapable of either thought or reaction at that moment as they tried to process what they were seeing. Elisa was the first to move and screamed "Mom" as she sprinted for the porch. Wes and Kristi slowly released their hands and locked eyes. The perfect ending had suddenly taken on a cruel twist.

ABOUT THE AUTHORS

This novel marks the inaugural collaboration between Brian and Randy Delaney, two brothers who bring distinctive perspectives to their storytelling. Brian's extensive travels during his career in the airline industry have endowed him with a profound global understanding of the human condition. Having forged connections with individuals from diverse backgrounds and cultures worldwide, he possesses a unique insight into the intricacies of the human spirit. Randy, with a background in literature and a multifaceted writing career spanning from sports journalism to children's literature, brings a wealth of literary expertise to their joint endeavors. His contributions include the authorship of children's books and the publication of numerous articles in esteemed trade journals and industry magazines.

Presently, Brian divides his time between his residences in Traverse City, MI, and Crystal River, FL, where he indulges his passion for long-distance cycling and continues to draw inspiration from his journeys. In contrast, Randy, a seasoned motorcyclist with over five decades of experience, navigates the country's backroads on his Harley from his home base in Pensacola, FL. As a former Special Forces veteran, Randy channels his sense of duty and patriotism by riding with The Patriot Guard Riders, a volunteer group dedicated to escorting deceased veterans on their final journey.